Concepts of the Self

Key Concepts

Barbara Adam, *Time*

Alan Aldridge, *Consumption*

Alan Aldridge, *The Market*

Colin Barnes and Geoff Mercer, *Disability*

Darin Barney, *The Network Society*

Mildred Blaxter, *Health*

Harry Brighouse, *Justice*

Steve Bruce, *Fundamentalism*

Margaret Canovan, *The People*

Alejandro Colás, *Empire*

Anthony Elliott, *Concepts of the Self*

Steve Fenton, *Ethnicity*

Michael Freeman, *Human Rights*

Russell Hardin, *Trust*

Fred Inglis, *Culture*

Jennifer Jackson Preece, *Minority Rights*

Paul Kelly, *Liberalism*

Anne Mette Kjær, *Governance*

Ruth Lister, *Poverty*

Jon Mandle, *Global Justice*

Michael Saward, *Democracy*

John Scott, *Power*

Anthony D. Smith, *Nationalism*

Stuart White, *Equality*

CONCEPTS OF THE SELF

Anthony Elliott

polity

First published in 2007 by Polity Press

Polity Press
65 Bridge Street
Cambridge CB2 1UR, UK

Polity Press
350 Main Street
Malden, MA 02148, USA

ISBN-13: 978-07456-3945-1
ISBN-13: 978-07456-3946-8 (pb)

A catalogue record for this book is available from the British Library.

Typeset in 10.5 on 12 pt Sabon
by SNP Best-set Typesetter Ltd, Hong Kong
Printed and bound in Great Britain by MPG Books Ltd, Bodmin, Cornwall

The publisher has used its best endeavours to ensure that the URLs for external websites referred to in this book are correct and active at the time of going to press. However, the publisher has no responsibility for the websites and can make no guarantee that a site will remain live or that the content is or will remain appropriate.

Every effort has been made to trace all copyright holders, but if any have been inadvertently overlooked the publishers will be pleased to include any necessary credits in any subsequent reprint or edition.

For further information on Polity, visit our website: www.polity.co.uk

Contents

Acknowledgements   viii

Introduction   1

The Arts of Self   7
Concepts of the Self   12
The Structure of the Book   24

1 Self, Society and Everyday Life   28

Self, Symbols and Others: Symbolic Interactionism   30
Presentations of Self: Goffman   37
Reflexivity and the Self: Giddens   44

2 The Repression of Self   53

Psychoanalysis and the Self   56
Culture and Repression   72

3 Technologies of the Self   85

Technologies of the Self: Foucault   88
Governmentality: New Technologies, New Selves   103

4 Self, Sexuality and Gender   112

Feminism and Psychoanalysis: Two Recent Views   112
The Politics of Gender Performance: Butler   124
Queer Theory: Contesting Self, Defying Gender   130

5 **The Postmodern Self**   138

All that is Modern Melts into Postmodern?   143
Strategies of the Self: Modern and Postmodern   153

Conclusion   162

Inner Depth, or Inside Out   162
Identity Politics, or Critique of Self   166
Afterword: Globalization, Postmodernization
    and New Individualism   169

Index   173

For Caoimhe

Acknowledgements

My thanks to everyone at Polity, and especially Andrea Drugan and Sarah Dancy, for assistance in preparing this second edition. Since the first edition appeared in 2001, I have been gratified to receive many unsolicited comments from students and lecturers in fields such as sociology, political science, cultural studies and psychology. As the book itself tries to demonstrate, there is no one disciplinary approach from which adequately to grasp the complexities of the self in our world of advanced globalization; on the contrary, only an interdisciplinary approach – the standpoint of social theory – can sufficiently scoop up recent theoretical developments surrounding subjectivity (from structuralism to psychoanalysis, feminism to postmodernism) in order to engage the concepts of self which are so fundamental to both public political life and the social sciences and humanities.

I should like to thank the many academics who read and commented upon the updating of the book. I should also like to thank my colleagues at the Department of Sociology at Flinders University for their support and encouragement of the research I conduct in social theory. Flinders has a long and distinguished tradition of innovation in social theory, and its abiding commitment to the public political relevance of sociology has made it an ideal environment in which to work.

The following people have provided invaluable assistance whilst working on this edition: Gerhard Boomgaarden, Daniel

Chaffee, Paul du Gay, Charles Lemert, Anthony Moran and Nick Stevenson. Finally, I should like to thank Nicola Geraghty, as well as Caoimhe and Oscar Elliott, for their help and for continuing to inspire my sociological imagination, both professional and practical. This book originally appeared around the time of Caoimhe's birth, and it always was her book: as I watch her navigate the rich territories of her world, I now realize it remains her book, more than ever.

Anthony Elliott
Adelaide

Introduction

With the soothing sound of the BBC sounding from her alarm clock at 6.00 am, Ronda wakes – like many the world over living in expensive cites of the West – to the latest news bulletin from digital radio. Listening to the morning headlines, she grabs her mobile phone to check any emails that came in overnight. A high-flying lawyer based in London, Ronda is working at present on a corporate takeover involving both British and American companies – and later in the day will fly to New York for further discussions on the deal. But it's coffee she needs first. Heading downstairs, she flicks on the LCD television inbuilt on the refrigerator in her minimalist kitchen and checks the international weather on ITV. Sitting down to coffee and a bagel, she scans the morning newspapers not only to see what's going on in the world but also to check the latest financial developments. All of this has taken about 15 minutes. The city is London, but it might just as easily be Los Angeles, Sydney, Singapore, Athens or Auckland.

Ronda's morning routine tells us a good deal about our changing world in these early days of the twenty-first century. Certainly it tells us about the rise of information and communications technology in recent times, but also about the changing nature of the self. For the global communications revolution has impacted profoundly on modern societies, and perhaps nowhere more so than in the everyday routines through which individuals forge and sustain a sense of self. Clearly, those like Ronda living in information-rich societies have an enormous degree of choice in accessing news and entertainment through the mass media. This explosion of global communications is crucial to the transformed nature of the self in various ways. First, an individual's use of mass media – from newspapers and digital radio to satellite television and the Internet – is not simply about the gathering of information – however important that might be. It informs – in a deeply symbolic way – our everyday activities and connections with others. What one gleans from the morning news, for example, provides fertile subject matter for various routine interactions in which the self is implicated – from discussions with friends in cafés to dialogue with fellow workers at the office.

Second, an individual who reads the morning newspaper is also caught up in a complicated process of self-definition and consumer identification. Whether one chooses to read *The Times*, the *Daily Mail* or *News of the World* – and indeed whether one reads the printed version or reads online – says a great deal about the relation between the self and broader socio-economic contexts. People can separate themselves from others – in actual, imagined and virtual ways – through reliance on the cultural status of media products. Consumer identification with media products often functions in a kind of make-believe way – 'I *only* read the *New York Times*' – but also profoundly influences the self-presentations of individuals. Indeed, for many people, this kind of brand loyalty is definitional of their 'ideal self' – the self that they would *like* to be.

Third, our routine engagement with the mass media implicates the self in a complex web of social, cultural and economic relationships that span the globe. Thanks to the transnational spread of new information technologies, our media-saturated society has created what the Canadian scholar Marshsall McLuhan terms a 'global village' – people increasingly define aspects of their self-identity, as well as memories of self, with reference to global media spectacles. In a world of intensive globalization, breaking news almost anywhere in the world is relayed instantaneously by the mass media. Such developments have not only provided for a much more interconnected world, but also redefine aspects of the constitution of the self with reference to other societies and other cultures. Where were you when the news of Princess Dianna's death broke? What were you doing on the morning of 9/11, when news of the planes that brought down the Twin Towers spread across the globe? More and more often, people are coming to define aspects of their self-experience – and particularly memories of the self – with reference to global mega-events. While social analysts still debate the pros and cons of the globalization of the media, there is growing evidence that our televisual world of 24/7 news updates and media spectacles is reshaping the self with postnational consequences. That is to say, the self is increasingly defined with reference to global forces, flows and networks – although whether people choose to embrace or deny such worldwide social transformations on a conscious level is an altogether separate issue.

Finally, the reshaping of the self through engagement with the mass media moves us to reflect on contemporary debates about modernity, postmodernism and, in particular, the much contested idea of a 'speeding-up' of the world. Some sociologists of the media have argued that today's good quality newspapers – such as the *Los Angeles Times* or the *Guardian* – contain as much information as an individual might have encountered over the course of their entire lifetime in a premodern society. This clearly raises issues about 'information overload' in modern societies; but it also raises complex questions concerning the self and its navigation of the myriad narratives and kaleidoscopic perspectives available through the mass media today. How do people forge a coherent sense of self against the expansive spread of information available through the mass media? How does the society of information overload impact upon processes of self-formation? These are issues that increasingly impact upon everyone today.

All these basic themes concerning changes affecting the self can, as I say, be inferred from the vignette of Ronda's hi-tech morning routine. There is little doubt that Ronda can be said to live a very privileged life, but there are aspects of her self-experience as described above which are increasingly prevalent and significant for people throughout the world – certainly in the expensive cities of the West. But, increasingly, such

personal and social changes also have globalizing consequences. As I try to demonstrate in this book, concepts of the
self have a key role to play in both the production of everyday
life and a central place in the social sciences. *Concepts of the
Self* is thus an attempt to make various social, cultural, political and psychological aspects of the self in our changing
world intelligible to a wide readership. As we will see throughout the book, concepts of the self have been studied by
philosophers and sociologists, by psychoanalysts as well as
cultural theorists. Almost all intellectual evaluations of the
self draw from, as well as feed back into, our everyday commonsense understandings of the self. This continual inter-
change between everyday and intellectual understandings of
the self is a key theme of the book.

Increasingly, many people today reflect on their sense of
self in terms of their private life – particularly as regards
friends, family, intimacy and sexuality. In the contemporary
world, selfhood is often experienced as a private affair – as
a matter of personal choice, design or project, as a defining
aspect of inner desires and dreams. Certainly, in our con-
sumer-driven culture in these early days of the twenty-first
century, identity is private and privatizing; everywhere, identity is sold as the means for personal happiness and freedom.
From the Nike culture of just-do-it to the micro made-to-
measure world of iPods, selfhood is advertised, televised and
talked about as the principal means for both joining and
enjoying the modern world. Many of the social theories of
identity that I examine in this book critically interrogate what
might be termed this *privatization of the self*. To think about
selfhood critically is to think beyond the illusions of a purely
private world, supposedly unaffected or cut off from the
wider social world. For we are all, no matter where we grew
up or what successes or otherwise we might have achieved in
our lives, exposed to *cultures* and *structures* in a profound
and ongoing sense. And nowhere more so than when we
think we are alone, when we think we are 'away' from the
world, when we think we act on the basis of our own 'private'
or unique sense of self. Yet this is not, as it may at first seem,
a completely cynical view of the self. Some of the social theories that we will look at in this book do indeed analyse the
riddles of self primarily in terms of wider social forces, such

as long-term historical processes or social structures. But other theorists of self take perhaps a more complex view, one that critically interrogates the whole relationship between private and public life. The personal life of the self, from this angle, is embedded in powerful unconscious forces, which are in turn deeply rooted in the ways of life of society.

In still another way, all social theories of the self turn on issues of control, capabilities and capacities. This is a more complex point, and the debate around it has involved some difficult terminology – but I think the essence of the issue can be easily summarized. Many sociologists talk about the self primarily in terms of the experience of *agency* – the degree of active involvement individuals have in shaping both their personal and cultural experience. In everyday life, we routinely engage in social practices – from buying the morning newspaper to taking the dog for an evening walk – in which, for the most part, we express agency in what we do. Self-management, self-shaping, self-stylization, engaging with other people: this is just how we give structure to our identities. As directors of our own lives, we draw upon emotional frames of memory and desire, as well as wider cultural and social resources, in fashioning the self. Expressions of personal agency – whether of writing a letter or uttering the words 'I love you' – are not something that happens through our actions alone (however much we sometimes think this is so). For practices of the self can also be experienced as forces impinging upon us – through the design of other people, the impact of cultural conventions and social practices, or the force of social processes and political institutions. Society then might be said to discipline and regulate the self, so that our deepest feelings about ourselves, as well as our beliefs about our identities, are shaped to their roots by broader social forces and cultural sensibilities. We may, for example, go to the gym fairly regularly in order to try to attain some ideal body shape (and, by implication, an ideal self), and we may do so because this really matters to us and it is experienced as a personal decision or choice. But in the social theories of self that we will examine in this book, there are always other puzzling social forces at work. There are always cultural or commercial factors influencing the self – for example, omnipresent media delivering never-ending images of ideal body-types as well as the selling of strategies to achieve such 'perfect bodies'.

This issue of the agency of the self is certainly a confounding puzzle, and one that often divides many of the social thinkers that we will examine in this book. In attempting to understand the lives of individuals, and of the role that society and culture plays in their lives, should we emphasize the practical knowledge of people? If so, to what extent? But what if 'practical knowledge' of the self is shaped to its roots by the power of the social bond? At the heart of these questions is an intriguing division which has arisen in the social sciences over the self-shaping of creative individuals, on the one hand, and the social regulation or control of selfhood on the other. The self has come to be viewed by some social analysts and cultural critics as an upshot of *cultural constraint* or *social exclusion*, an approach which, as we will see, focuses on the status of social forces and institutional dynamics. For other critics, the self can only be adequately understood by grasping the *creativity of action*, focusing in particular on personal agency and autonomy. The concept of the reflective, reasoning self has been central to many schools of thought in the social sciences, and yet an emphasis on human agency varies considerably depending on whether we are discussing sociological, psychoanalytic, post-structuralist, feminist or postmodern approaches. Sociological theories, for example, tend to emphasize how our sense of self is shaped by one or another institution or cultural form in the larger society, how we build up notions of the self and other selves as social constructions, and how concepts of the self play a central role in the constitution and reproduction of social networks. Psychoanalytic theories, by contrast, put the emphasis on the organization of our internal worlds, on the emotional conflicts of identity, and on the power of the individual to create, maintain and transform relations between the self and others. Concepts of the self emerging from these traditions of thought – that is, sociology and psychoanalysis – have very different ways of conceptualizing how individuals cope with the burdens of self in their day-to-day lives. Sociologists and psychoanalytic critics deal with this issue, as I shall discuss in the chapters that follow, by prioritizing either social forces or individuals in conceptualizing the self.

The relation between identity and society is therefore fundamental to thinking about the self. But there are also other themes of key significance in approaching concepts of the self. Just as social theory divides over prioritizing either social or individual experience in the constitution of the self, so too issues over unity and fragmentation, continuity and difference, rationality and passion, gender and sexuality, come strongly into focus. In the psychoanalytic reading of self and personal identity, for example, individual strivings, desires and actions are grasped as *self-divided*, torn between that part of the mind that is conscious, rational and reflexive, and the unconscious motivations that lurk within us, but of which we are dimly aware. Postmodern theory shifts these conflicts of identity up a gear, arguing for the multiplication of narratives of self as a site for reconfiguring relations between society, culture and knowledge.

The Arts of Self

A radio station to which I sometimes listen recently ran a competition called 'The New You'. The competition was designed for 'losers': people with recurring difficulties in their personal and intimate lives. To enter, it was necessary to describe on radio some embarrassing private situation or circumstance – for instance, something going horribly wrong on a first date, falling in love with your best friend's partner, or making a personal gaffe at work. The act of discussing one's personal embarrassment on radio placed the entrant in line for a play-off with other 'losers'. The final winner – in this case the 'grand loser' – took home prizes with which to 'remake his or her identity'. The winning prize consisted of a car, clothes, holiday and cash. I raise the radio competition because it offers an interesting example, I think, of some core links between popular culture and dominant conceptions of the self. For the defining outlook pervading the competition seemed to be that individuals are relatively free to experiment with their sense of identity. The self, in this view, becomes a matter of choice and risk. If you are willing to take identity risks – in this case, to tell a wider public about some aspect of your intimate life – then you do not have to be a loser. The radio competition was conducted, of course, in a spirit of light-heartedness. Yet it remains suggestive of deep cultural assumptions governing how we see the self: namely, that it is linked to role-playing, gender, choice, risk and, above all, the realm of consumption.

There are profound connections between the cultural assumptions informing 'The New You' competition. on the one hand, and, on the other, concepts of the self in the social sciences and humanities today. Selfhood is flexible, fractured, fragmented, decentred and brittle: such a conception of individual identity is probably the central outlook in current social and political thought. As the pace, intensity and complexity of contemporary culture accelerate, so too does the self become increasingly dispersed. Displaced and dislocated within the wider global frame of post-industrial capitalism, the individual self turns increasingly to consumption, leisure and travel in order to give substance to everyday life. Or so some have forcefully argued. Many other authors, for a variety of reasons that we will examine, remain sceptical of such a portrait of the self. I shall discuss shortly the complex, and often unintended, ways in which the academic study of the self can, of itself, shape the cultural know-how and resources of the broader society. At this point it is worth briefly noting some core concepts of the self, some of them social science ones, which influence our everyday understandings of personal experience and individual identity.

In day-to-day life, we implicitly assume, and act on the basis, that individuals have a 'sense of self'. We refer to people as selves; we recognize that most people, most of the time, deploy commonsense understandings of personal and social experience in order to manage the routine nature of their social worlds. We recognize that making sense of lives is often difficult, sometimes confusing, and that we are recurrently ambivalent about the coherence of our sense of personal identity. This mysterious terrain of our social and cultural life is, sociologically speaking, at the core of the arts of self. There is very little that goes on in daily social life that is not, in some very basic sense, conditioned, structured or dependent upon such fabrications of the self. The making, remaking and transformation of self-experience are fundamental to these arts. Things change; people change. Societal ambivalence and private torment lead us to see that identity is fluid, not fixed once and for all. In the terms of a key socio-logical tradition that will be discussed later, the self is a *symbolic project* that the individual actively and creatively forges. The self can be understood as a symbolic project in the sense that people routinely refer to their sense of identity as a guiding orientation to their lives, to other people, and to the broader society. In this sense, individuals can be said to use *practical knowledge* as a means of producing and reproducing their defining sense of self.

Some critics reject the idea that practical knowledge is an essential characteristic of the self. Some critics argue that, as sociologists or social critics, we needn't concern ourselves with the intricate settings and assumptions that people bring to their presentations of self; rather, the self can instead be studied as an *object*, without reference to the interpretations that individuals make about their own lives or their views about the wider social world. This is not a view I share. Indeed, one argument I develop throughout this book is that the self cannot be adequately studied in isolation from the interpretations that individuals make about themselves, others and society. Charles Taylor develops this point in an interest-ing fashion:

> We are selves only in that certain issues matter for us. What I am as a self, my identity, is essentially defined by the way things have significance for me. And as has been widely dis-cussed, these things have significance for me, and the issue of my identity is worked out, only through a language of inter-pretation which I have come to accept as a valid articulation of these issues. To ask what a person is, in abstraction from his or her self-interpretations, is to ask a fundamentally mis-guided question, one to which there couldn't in principle be an answer. . . . We are not selves in the way that we are organ-isms, or we don't have selves in the way we have hearts and livers. We are living beings with these organs quite indepen-dently of our self-understandings or interpretations, or the meanings things have for us. But we are only selves insofar as we move in a certain space of questions. (Charles Taylor, *Sources of the Self*, Cambridge, Mass.: Harvard UP, 1990, p. 34)

The self, on this view, is fashioned from individuals regularly appraising what it is they do (watching TV, going shopping, staying 'in') as a means of actually performing such activities. All selfhood has a 'recursive' or 'reflexive' quality to it, as we will see in chapter 1 when examining the sociology of the self. The self is recursive or reflexive to the degree that people constantly monitor, or watch, their own activities, thoughts or emotions as a means of *generating* these aspects of their identity.

To emphasize the significance of an individual's interpretations about their own sense of selfhood, however, is not to suggest that people can ever fully know all there is to know about the conditions of their lives. Many authors have argued that selfhood, in a sense, *fails*; such accounts emphasize that the stories we tell about ourselves fall short of the deeper truth of lived experience. The founding father of psychoanalysis, Sigmund Freud, is perhaps the central figure here. Freud's theory of a self dislocated and fractured by repressed desire suggests that self-experience is radically divided, or split, between conscious, rational thought on the one hand and unconscious desire, fantasies and memories on the other. The Freudian conception of unconscious desire and motivation has entered sociology, political science, feminism and philosophy in important ways, principally in connection with the study of the dividing line between presentations and pathologies of the self. Psychoanalytic theories of the self are rich and challenging not only because they dethrone commonsense understandings of individual intentions and reasoning; what is valuable in psychoanalytic concepts of the self is the stress on emotional dynamics of loss, longing and mourning.

This is not to say that the self is only fashioned, as it were, from the inside out. In forging a sense of self, individuals routinely draw from social influences, and maintain their sense of self through cultural resources. Social practices, cultural conventions and political relations are a constitutive backdrop for the staging of self-identity. But even this formulation is perhaps inadequate. The self is not simply 'influenced' by the external world, since the self cannot be set apart from the social, cultural, political and historical contexts in which it is embedded. Social processes in part constitute, and so in a sense are internal to, the self. Neither internal nor external frames of reference should be privileged; all forms of identity are astonishingly imaginative fabrications of the private and public, personal and political, individual and historical.

We almost never think about the critical knowledge, including that of social science, which feeds into and contributes to our practical understanding of the self. And yet the knowledge skills that inform our personal repertoires of the self are shaped to their roots by academic and social forces. The British sociologist Anthony Giddens has coined the term 'double hermeneutic' to refer to the application of lay knowledge to the technical language of the social sciences, as well as the utility of social science findings to the reality of a person's day-to-day life. While philosophers of the social sciences have largely concentrated their energies on the ways in which lay concepts necessarily intrude into the claims of science, Giddens has instead focused, appropriately enough for a sociologist, on how social science concepts routinely enter our lives and help redefine them. According to Giddens, the language of economics, or political science, or sociology not only provides knowledge that informs in useful and edifying ways. In addition, the language of social science creates knowledge in a much more profound sense, as the utility of this knowledge becomes basic to the economies, polities and societies of the contemporary epoch. The discourse of economics, for example, enters constitutively into the very social world it describes: the usage of terms like 'liquidity' and 'inflation' are in some part mastered, on the level of practical consciousness, by people going about their day-to-day affairs within modern economies; even though individuals might not be able to articulate the logical principles governing liquidity or inflation discursively, those same individuals exhibit a practical knowledge of such concepts whenever the bank is visited or goods are purchased prior to a price rise. To study some aspect of social life implies for Giddens that the findings of social science can be incorporated into the social practices that they are, in a sense, about.

Giddens's claim that the practical impact of the social sciences is inescapable carries important consequences and implications for studying the self. Because the self is not a fixed entity, but is rather actively constructed, individuals are capable of incorporating and modifying knowledge that influences their sense of personal identity. Consider, for example, the notion of lifestyles. Today, lifestyles are a crucial aspect of both self-identity and social organization. Once the preserve of the rich and famous, the mass marketing of lifestyles through advertising has increasingly opened identity out to the realms of choice, individuality, aesthetics, disposable income and consumption. Interestingly enough, however, the word 'lifestyle' once denoted something very different. The *Oxford English Dictionary* lists the psychologist Alfred Adler as coining the term in 1929. Adler used the notion of lifestyle to describe a person's essential character structure as established in early childhood. More specifically, he deployed it in order to account for personal behaviour and emotional reactions throughout the life-cycle. He argued that the core style of life is founded in the first four or five years of childhood, and that a fragment of memory preserves the motives of a lifestyle for an individual. In time, Adler's notion of lifestyle became incorporated into common stocks of knowledge by which individuals in the wider society pursue their personal and practical activities. This knowledge, modified as it was by advertisers and the market, fostered an active, imaginative (and no doubt, at times, also a somewhat coercive) restructuring of self-experience in terms of lifestyle pursuits and niche subcultures. Those who have drawn from this knowledge might never have heard of Alfred Adler, but his influence over modern lifestyles and the construction of the self has been immense – even though it has been in a fashion that he could not have foreseen, or (one suspects) approved. The broader point to note, at this stage, is that the relationship between professional and practical concepts of the self – that is, between academic and popular understandings of personal identity – is crucial to many of the social theories I discuss. How conceptual perspectives on the self mediate our everyday understandings of personal identity is a theme I shall examine in some detail.

Concepts of the Self

The emerging direction of contemporary social theory is perhaps nowhere more evident than in the attention it lavishes upon the nature of the self, self-identity and individual subjectivity. Questions concerning the social construction of the self; debates pertaining to the symbolic materials through which individuals weave narratives of the self; issues relating to the role that self-formation plays in the reproduction or disruption of culture and society: such questions, debates and issues have become increasingly prominent in the social sciences in recent decades. For those working within sociology, for example, the topic of the self has provided an opportunity for re-examining the relation between the individual and society, an opportunity to detail the myriad ways in which individuals are constituted as identities or subjects who interact in a socially structured world of people, relationships and institutions. The issues at stake in the construction of the self are quite different for feminist writers, who are instead concerned with connecting processes of self-formation to distinctions of gender, sexuality and desire. The challenge for authors drawing from contemporary conceptions of postmodernism, by way of further comparison, is to estimate the degree to which the self may be fragmenting or breaking down, as well as assessing the psychological and cultural contours of postmodern selfhood. In all these approaches, the turn to the self provides critical perspectives on the present age as well as an important source of understanding concerning transformations of knowledge, culture and society.

Selfhood emerges as a complex term as a result of these various theoretical interventions, and one of the central concerns of *Concepts of the Self* is the discrimination of different meanings relating to the self, in order to introduce the beginning reader to the contemporary debates around it. What needs to be stressed at the outset is that different social theories adopt alternative orientations to mapping the complexities of personal experience, such that the conceptualization of selfhood is squarely pitched between those who deny the agency of human subjects and argue in favour of the person's determination by social structures, on the one hand, and those who celebrate the authenticity and creativity of the self, on the other. As a result, the language used by social theorists and social scientists to analyse selfhood varies considerably: sometimes theorists refer to 'identity', sometimes to 'the subject' or 'subjectivity', and sometimes simply to 'the self'.

These terminological differences are not always especially significant, primarily because these terms can all be said to denote a concern with the subjectivity of the individual. However, others argue that such terminological differences are worth close attention, if only because they reflect deep historical and political transitions. For example, it can plausibly be argued that the concepts of 'the self' and 'identity', though similar, are not coextensive, since there are forms of identity which are not based on the self, namely, forms of collective identity, such as nationalist identities. In this reading, collective identity gains its power through the establishment and recognition of common interests, built upon forms of solidarity involving battles over, say, social exclusion, nation, class and the like. Similarly, the self is also shaped and defined against the backdrop of such political and public forces; yet the fabrication of the self, psychologically and emotionally, is rightly understood to involve something more subjective, particularly in the ways in which desire, emotion and feeling influence the conscious and unconscious experience of sexuality, gender, race and ethnicity.

One might add, though this is much debated, that the influence of traditional identity categories has dramatically loosened in our age of light mobility, liquid experiences and dispersed commitments. In present-day society, as we will examine in some detail in the Conclusion, private grievances and emotional anxieties connect less and less with the framing of collective identities; in more and more cases, private troubles remain *private*. Contemporary hopes and dreads, so we are repeatedly told by popular culture and the mass media, are something to be experienced by each individual alone. Indeed there are good reasons, I shall argue, to see a general shift from identity to the self as a new marker of our times – in terms of both engagement with individual experience and the wider world, but also as concerns new forms of domination and exploitation.

I shall not trace the nuances of these conceptual differences here; the philosophical history of subjectivity has been extensively discussed elsewhere (see Anthony Cascardi, *The Subject of Modernity*, Cambridge University Press, 1992; Seyla Benhabib, *Situating the Self*, Cambridge: Polity, 1992). But I do want to say something in this Introduction, however briefly, about versions of the self in current sociology and social theory.

No idea is more unstable, flexible or pliable in contemporary social theory than that of the self. But what, exactly, is the self? We all have a sense of self-identity; we all perform 'selves' in the rituals of daily life; we all interact with other 'selves'. Yet how is the self rendered identical to itself? And why do our society and cultural life privilege *continuity* at the level of the self? We in the West – to the extent that one can use the term 'We', which, as we will see, is itself an issue arising from the politics of self – have been inculcated in a philosophy that holds that 'selfhood is sameness', that there is such a thing as continuity of identity over time and for all time. Strictly speaking, such philosophy goes back as far as Descartes: 'I think, therefore I am'. It is here that the essence of the classical idea of consciousness of self as a sure foundation for knowledge and social action is to be found. Historically speaking, however, even such rarefied, philosophical ideas of the self altered in meaning from time to time and place to place. Confidence in some minimal degree of self-continuity – 'I am the same self as I was yesterday' – has been, of course, an essential precondition for all successful living. But only the very few, either because of extraordinary privilege or lack of interest in the surrounding world, could fail ever to question their own security of self. Few could avoid the interpersonal situations that arose – day-in and day-out – wherein the uncertainty of social life disturbed. To convert the whole fabric of social relations into the engine of self-constitution is, however, a tricky business – as the nineteenth-century psychologist William James most powerfully underscored. For if the self depends for its security on its surrounding social relations, then this seems to deny to identity the certitude many thought existed. As James noted, if the individual has as many selves as there are persons who recognize him or her, then how can that self function 'the same' as it did yesterday? It certainly makes our selfhood appear less fixed, or more psychologically flexible, than some dominant Western worldviews seem to have assumed. From this angle, the word 'self' means both fixed and pliable. Hence much of the study of the self has passed through these over-lapping societal strands of continuity and discontinuity – for example George Herbert Mead, as we will see in the opening chapter, was concerned to track the work of what he termed the 'I' in roping the social self, or 'me', under some form of control from its various cultural interactions.

In the forms most familiar to our own age, however, the flourishing of concepts of the self is really a product of various global transformations that unfolded from about the early 1960s through to the postmodern 1980s and 1990s. For by the 1960s – when the security and serenity of the post-Second World War economic boom that had prevailed throughout North America and much of the world drew to a close, replaced by the era of the Vietnam War, the emergent decolonizing and civil rights movements as well as feminist politics and the sexual revolution – identity had broken with images of sameness, continuity, regularity and repetition. Selfhood was now also coming to mean disaffection, rebellion, discontinuity and difference. Revolution was spreading throughout social life, with student rebellions on campuses across the United States and a dramatic student and worker uprising in France that came close to toppling the de Gaulle government. There were anxieties over race too, in Europe and the American South, in Africa, the Latin Americas and Asia, and a politics of cultural revolution took hold in everything from feminism to Black Power. Selfhood in the sense of excluded histories, displaced narratives, marginalized lives and oppressed identities was fundamental to the attempts of people – women, gays, blacks and subalterns of all kinds – to question the status quo and change the direction of society. This was, in short, the era of 'identity crisis' (as Erik Erikson described it), in which the illusion of traditional European individualism was shattered, the military and economic might of America deeply questioned, and the formerly repressed energies of new social movement activists and critics now burst into full cultural expression. In all of this – the shift from social conformity to cultural revolution – we find traces of the intellectual thought of many key theorists of the self which are examined throughout this book. Indeed, the idea of a cultural revolution of the structures of everyday life, sexuality, gender, the family, race relations and, in fact, the whole fabric of social relations depended in various ways upon the 'rewriting' of the self articulated by Wilhelm Reich,

Herbert Marcuse, Erving Goffman, Jacques Lacan, Michel Foucault and various other feminist, structuralist and postmodern social theorists.

This is not to say, however, that the cultural revolts of the 1960s arose as an upshot of certain radical ideas then circulating throughout universities. Those involved in various branches of the emergent identity politics of the 1960s and 1970s, from feminism to decolonization movements, might never have done more than glance at Herbert Marcuse's photograph on the cover of *Time* magazine (if indeed they did that), or might well have thought that psychoanalysis was nothing more than a variant of other psychological therapies. My point is not to suggest some one-way impress of academic ideas upon the turmoil of the times. So what is the significance of these social theorists of the self? It consists, I suggest, in the critical self-reflection promoted by these radical interrogations of the self. Radical politics, of whatever ideological kind, comes about when people are led into a new self-confrontation with their own lives. The social theories of the self that flourished during the 1960s and escalated throughout the 1970s, only to falter and mutate into a postmodern dismantling of the self in the 1980s and 1990s, were just such a challenge to the prevailing social order. Jacques Lacan's Freudian decentring of the self, Herbert Marcuse's suggestive twinning of sociality and the unconscious, Michel Foucault's brilliant interrogations of technologies of lived experience, Judith Butler's feminist redrafting of the intricate connections between gender and sexuality: all these theoretical accounts of the self, as we shall examine in this book, have promoted a suspicion of identity norms, given values, established hierarchies and traditional social practices.

In terms of political transformations and cultural shifts, whether we are considering the heady days of cultural revolution from the 1960s or postmodern subversions of identity during the 1980s and 1990s, there are various sociological consequences which have followed from these deconstructions and reconstructions of the self in social theory. What gradually took place from the late 1960s onwards, when identity politics defined itself increasingly as a mass political movement, partly as a result of novel theoretical departures and innovations and partly as a consequence of new forms of political action, was a radical shift in our whole cultural vocabulary for understanding the inner world of the self, individual experience and personal identity. That is to say, changing conceptions of the self at the level of the academy and the public sphere inevitably intruded into the realms of daily life and culture. Some have argued, for example, that the women's movement in its contemporary forms would not have had the same impact without a body of sophisticated feminist theory which arose out of the political upheavals and cultural turmoils of the 1960s and 1970s – a body of thought which, in turn, was indebted to changing conceptions of the individual subject and personal identity in the social sciences and humanities. Certainly the heavily politicized culture of the 1960s and early 1970s, in which a new stress on personal experimentation, self-transformation, lifestyle and identity politics emerged, penetrated deeply into the tissues of cultural practice and everyday life. Politics, as a result, revolved more and more around the personal; the personal, having been previously cast off to the realm of the 'private', in other words, was now to be reinserted into the political. This was obviously true of feminism, and especially so in the works of various feminist theorists we consider later in this book, such as Simone de Beauvoir, Nancy Chodorow, Julia Kristeva and Judith Butler. But it was also true of other forms of self-politics, from the civil rights movement to queer theory. Not all were convinced, however, by such attempts to deepen and enrich politics through an engagement with the personal. Some critics argued, for example, that the whole concept of self had become over-inflated – so much so that issues of human agency and radical politics were, in turn, cut loose from social and historical forces altogether. This is not a view I share, for reasons that will become apparent throughout this book. At any rate, to emphasize the active, creative character of the self is not to imply that identity is culturally or politically unconditioned. On the contrary, the turn to the self in social theory has powerfully underscored that racialized, hybridized, sexualized and gendered productions of identity are intimately interwoven with complex forces of economic disadvantage, social marginalization and political exclusion.

The turn to the self arises, then, as a central preoccupation of the social sciences and humanities for a whole range of intellectual and political reasons, not least to comprehend the links between the individual construction of identity as an active, ongoing task (what sociologists call 'the symbolic project of the self') on the one hand, and processes of subjection to dominant ideologies and systems of meaning on the other. This is not, it should be said, to equate selfhood and subjection – although much critical social research of the late 1970s and 1980s certainly sought to theorize the self as a product of linguistic or symbolic systems which precede and shape it. This was the much celebrated 'decentring of the subject', based upon a heady blend of post-structuralism, discourse theory and psychoanalysis. While I am not able to consider all aspects of this complex philosophical debate in the pages that follow, I do focus on two seminal approaches to the self arising from the 'linguistic turn' in social science – namely, Lacan's 'return to Freud' (in chapter 2) and Foucault's technologies of self (in chapter 3).

Meanwhile, the arrival of the postmodern 1980s brought with it a further shift in conceptions of self. As globalization assumed a central place in the transformation of modern societies, especially in the areas of economics, politics, culture and communication, it became increasingly evident that a liberationist identity politics – where the recovery of excluded sexual, racial or other subaltern identities would mysteriously permit the flourishing of some previously repressed, fully formed self – contained various theoretical ambiguities and some full-blown political contradictions. The marginalized, volatile, constructed identities championed by the advocates of 1970s identity politics now appeared as more in harmony or collusion with market forces and the consumerist imperatives of advanced capitalism than as a discordant or oppositional social force. Meanwhile, new pressing political issues, including mass migration, multiculturalism, cultural Americanization and rampant consumerism, forced their way onto the political agenda, which in turn bred new social theories of the relation between self and society. At the political level, new forms of political resistance – from peace and ecology movements to human rights and citizenship campaigns –

raised anew the question of human agency and the creative dimension of social action. At the theoretical level, this led to the in-depth critique of the more negative or pessimistic elements of theories of identity formation in European social theory and philosophy. In particular, questions concerning the individual's capabilities for autonomous thought, independent reflection and transformative social practices emerged as politically important. In the face of these changes, another terminological shift occurred, one from the analysis of subjectivity and individual subjection to the study of the creative dimensions of the self.

The self, therefore, becomes a vital preoccupation of the contemporary age for a whole series of practical, political reasons. The impact of identity politics looms large in this context. Struggles over the politics of identity have intensified dramatically over the last couple of decades, with issues concerning gender, sexuality, race, ethnicity, multiculturalism, class and cultural style moving to the fore in public and intellectual debate. The socio-cultural horizon of identity politics – premised upon new conceptual strategies for both the theorization and the transformation of self – has provided important understandings of particular forms of oppression and domination suffered by specific groups, including women, lesbians and gay men, African-Americans and other stigmatized identities. Identity politics has produced cultural and strategic perspectives, concerned with the development of alternative concepts of the self, different narratives of identity and emancipatory strategies for mobilizing individuals and groups against oppressive practices, cultures and institutions. Questioning the universal categories that have long been deployed to unite identities in the name of liberation (such as truth, equality and justice), the struggle over identity politics has instead focused on the creation of the self, the articulation of cultural style and the production of fluid alliances for specific political interventions in concrete social processes.

Over the past several decades. what highlighted the topic of identity more than any other theoretical and political current, at least in terms of placing it most centrally on the agenda for cultural politics, was feminism. In advancing the slogan that the personal is always political, feminism effected a switch from institutional politics to cultural politics. Recasting everyday life as a terrain of struggle in the reproduction of unequal power relations, feminists focused on the historical interplay of sexuality, sex and gender in analysing constructions and contradictions of personal identity and the self. Since the eruption of women's liberation and the sexual revolution at the close of the 1960s, the conceptual and political strategies of feminism have shifted from the analysis of male domination, understood in terms of patriarchy, to the study of more localized forces for grasping divisions and differences across sexual life. Indeed, much concentration has been devoted to conflicts between women themselves in recent feminist debate. Today, in an age that is supposedly post-political, feminism has thrived (or so some have argued) on the demise of universalist arguments for the political and economic transformation of gender relations in favour of lifestyle and identity politics, with the stress on prioritizing multiple selves, cultural differences and gender instability. Alongside the rise of various new feminisms (including black and Third World women's groups), the period has also witnessed other forms of broadly transformative identity politics, from ecology and peace movements to forums for the survivors of domestic and sexual violence, from postcolonialist identities to the creation of transnational human rights organizations. In the process, the analysis of the self has been recast, from derivative of *political structures* or *social practices* towards *identity*, *information* and *images* as sites of possible restructuring for interpersonal relations and public life.

Identity politics is thus enormously wide-ranging in scope, and has bred a multitude of cultural forms and theoretical systems. This book discusses the provocative dialogue between identity politics scholarship and cultural activism, though the main focus concerns discriminating between different concepts of self that have entered popular and political discourse. The attempt to theorize explicitly the place of selfhood and identity within politics and culture has deepened in recent times, as social theorists and cultural analysts have turned to Freud, Marcuse, Lasch, Kristeva, Butler and others in order to develop a more sophisticated understanding of individual subjectivity in an age of pervasive globalization. In contemporary social theory, the cultures and conflicts of identity loom large, with the fragilities of personal experience and the self viewed as central to critical conversation concerning social practice and political transformation.

As a result of these conceptual developments and transformations, a number of social issues relating to identity politics arise. For many commentators, identity politics is valuable precisely because it draws attention to new cultural forms of social integration and conflict experienced at the level of the self – such as the search for cultural style and personal identity in consumerism, new information technologies, or alternative sub-cultures and movements. The importance of concepts of self and identity to critical discourse, according to these commentators, is deeply bound up with politics in the widest sense. That is to say, identity politics reflects not a turning away from public life, but rather expresses genuine global reach in inspiring progressive and transformative politics. The American sociologist Charles Lemert writes of the link between identity and politics thus:

> It is surely not by coincidence that the debates over the meaning of social identity are most viciously engaged at the very time when changes in world politics have provoked a related but no less urgent debate. The two entail each other. As the world changes according to indecipherable laws, identity becomes every bit as unstable a social thing as the suddenly decentred world economic system. Once an established world system begins to decompose, social instability seems to move with chaotic effect from the smallest to the greatest parts. It is obvious that the destabilizing of the modern world is associated with a curious, but undeniable, energizing of identity as the topic of widespread political interest. (Charles Lemert, *Postmodernism is not what You Think*, Oxford: Blackwell, 1997, p. 128)

Lemert's comments are suggestive, and underline the connections between such social forces as mass migration, the multicultural nation, the influence of the mass media, and American cultural standardization on the one hand, and the deep questioning (or, as Lemert says, energizing) of personal identity and the self on the other. This interconnection of global forces and personal dispositions is fundamental to understanding increased anxieties and controversies over the self in recent times. In the current intellectual climate, it is routinely claimed that the multiple sites of subjectivity – sexuality, gender, race, class, culture and power – refuse containment within institutionalized systems or structures. The self is portrayed as a resistant element to ordered structures, as that which gives the slip to theoretical and analytical categorization. In this reading, the self is radical and subversive, a subjective source of challenge to received social meanings. Yet if the self has loomed large in contemporary social theory, it is partly because identity infuses a wide variety of new social knowledges, from psychoanalysis to feminism to postmodernism. From this angle, concepts of the self are central to emerging forms of political struggle; such concepts inform, and indeed help constitute, subjective forms of resistance to regimes of power, in everything from signs and sexuality to ideology and international relations.

For other critics, however, identity politics is hardly energizing at all. According to this critique, identity politics deflects attention from the core political and institutional issues of the times, reducing politics to a solitary, individualistic search for personal identity. Politics in the sense of identity preoccupations leads to the elevation of individual choice over collective action, and prioritizes individualism over traditional collective means of political activity. The result is a kind of *anti-political politics*, one that promotes the privatization of public concerns. This leads modern women and men to imagine that problems of identity are, first and foremost, matters for individual attention and personal solution; the culture of identity politics is increasingly made up of isolated and isolating voices, with few cultural resources available for connecting personal troubles to public issues. In short, some worry that identity politics is too closed in on itself, unconcerned with wider political solidarity, and too intolerant and defensive properly to grasp how political demands for recognition and respect relate to oppressions of the wider political system. While it may be the case that questions concerning the constitution of the self have been linked to radical politics (as in, say, sexual politics or postcolonialism), it is much less clear that attention to the subjective aspects of social experience is always inherently subversive. Indeed, the opposite might be true. Some critics argue that the advanced capitalist order is so drenched with consumerist signs, codes and messages that the self is now, in effect, fully regulated by dominant social interests in advance. From this angle concentration upon the self is part of the political problem, not the solution.

Important differences regarding the nature of the self and self-experience are at stake in such evaluations of identity politics, and I shall look at the cultural gains and losses of contemporary debates around the paradoxes of self. In using conflicts over the self as my central reference point, I shall examine a range of cultural anxieties that have informed the language of self in sociological theories, in psychoanalytic readings, in recent post-structuralist (especially Foucauldian) theory and in feminist and postmodern critiques. This is a book about such social theories and their impact upon how we see the self.

The Structure of the Book

The chapters that follow are designed to introduce students to concepts and theories of the self within the social sciences. The book aims to examine critically the ideas, concepts and theories of the self that are used in social analysis while also discussing key areas in which such approaches have produced elucidation of the experience of self-identity, selfhood and personal identity.

Chapter 1 looks at how the self has entered sociology. The chapter introduces three powerful sociological approaches to understanding how the self is constituted and constructed in the social world. How do people draw on symbols and symbolic material to fashion a sense of self? How do they live a narrative of self-identity that is actively constructed and reconstructed in the course of a life trajectory? In addressing these questions, I pay close attention to George Herbert Mead's theories on the emergence of the self, and I also consider the ways in which his ideas have been developed in the sociological tradition of symbolic interactionism. The extremely subtle distinctions we often make in developing shared understandings about self-identity, as elucidated in the sociological writings of Erving Goffman, are also examined in this chapter. Finally, the chapter addresses the wider field of social theory and considers how self-identity links to social influences that are increasingly global in their implications and consequences. Here the writings of the British sociologist Anthony Giddens are discussed and critically evaluated.

Chapter 2 concentrates on psychoanalytic concepts of the self, with Freud's theory of the unconscious a major theme. The chapter is centrally concerned with the inner world of the self – the internal conflicts and unacceptable desires excluded from the conscious mind through processes of displacement, denial and repression. At the very least, Freud shows us that there is always a considerable gap between our ideal and real selves, the space between the private self and social identity. Strangeness, foreignness, otherness, ambivalence, incompleteness and insufficiency: at the core of Freud's theory of the unconscious are both forbidding and forbidden desires; the unconscious escapes explanation in terms of rationality or logic, and radically revises our commonsense understandings of the self as knowable, predictable and controlled; the repressed unconscious represents, in Freud's view, the most awesome stumbling block on the self's march to self-understanding and self-knowledge. Such riddles of the psyche as deciphered by Freud have proved attractive to various cultural analysts and social theorists interested in tracking the fate of the individual self in contemporary culture. From the writings of German critical theorist Herbert Marcuse to the Slovenian cultural critic Slavoj Žižek, the Freudian conception of self has been at the centre of radical social criticism, and my discussion in this chapter traces both the conceptual gains and the blind alleys of psychoanalytic scholarship.

The cultural regulations governing the manner in which individuals construct their identities against an array of social differences has long been a preoccupation of authors influenced by structural forms of analysis. Language is assumed to be at the core of the relation between self and society in structuralist-inspired social theory, specifically the organizing principles of personal identity on the one hand and social differences on the other. Chapter 3 examines the contribution of the French philosopher and historian Michel Foucault to the analysis of the self, power and language or discourse. Foucault's attempts to identify the systems of power through which individuals imprison themselves at the level of the self and individual subjectivity are discussed. His original argument that the relationship of the individual to society and history can be traced to a whole technology of the self is critically appraised, as is his emphasis on modern forms of psychotherapy for the coercive management of the self. The chapter concludes by considering the work of other scholars influenced by Foucault, including the so-called school of governmentalities, for theorizing the relation between self and society.

Chapter 4 focuses on the nature of gender and its relation to the self. Feminism holds that the social world is pervaded by gender, that men and women are socialized into distinct patterns of relating to each other, and that masculine and feminine senses of self are tied to asymmetrical relations of gender power. How is gender power reproduced at the level of the self? How do men and women acquire a distinct sense of masculine or feminine gender identity? The writings of two feminists strongly influenced by psychoanalysis, Nancy Chodorow and Julia Kristeva, are critically examined against this backdrop. I look in particular at the very different concepts of the self articulated by Chodorow and Kristeva, and compare their blending of feminism and psychoanalysis. Gender is also at the heart of contemporary anxiety about sexual choice, erotic orientation, and the bridging of sexuality and the performance or enactment of gender. The work of the radical sexual feminist, Judith Butler, on strategies for the subversion of gender identity is discussed in this context, and the chapter concludes with a discussion of recent gay and lesbian scholarship on the self as well a critical evaluation of queer theory.

Interpretations of the search for self-identity tend to divide around the issue of the extension of global social processes to everyday life and the impact of new communication technologies and mass-consumer cultures upon the personalized contexts in which experience is constituted. Some see the self in the contemporary epoch as increasingly frail, fractured and fragmented. Just as traditional forms of social integration have broken down, so also does the self. In an age of global capitalism and media saturation, the self dissolves. Others have reached a similar conclusion, but see the end result differently: not so much a dissolution as a rebirth – the emergence of new, postmodern forms of experience and identity. The debate about postmodernity is taken up in chapter 5. There I address the issue of why postmodernism is at once so emotionally exhilarating and disturbing for current experiences of selfhood. In an era where global changes in employment, leisure, knowledge, media production and intimacy are increasingly rapid and disruptive, new challenges and new burdens arise for personal identity and the self.

A final remark about the scope of this book. I have tried to develop in the pages that follow a concise introduction to some of the major concepts and theories of the self in contemporary social theory and social science. The book is not intended as an exhaustive discussion of the topic; in analysing the major theories of self in social theory today – from psychoanalysis and queer theory to Foucauldian and postmodern approaches – I have tried to keep the discussion lively and concise, and this means some sacrifice in respect of detail and complexity. Nonetheless, my hope is that the reader finds this critical introduction to the self substantial and engaging. If the reader is encouraged to delve deeper in current debates over the self as a consequence of this book, then its purpose will have been served.

1
Self, Society and Everyday Life

Overlooking the garden of their suburban house on a lovely summer's day, a man and woman talk quietly. Both regularly look over to where their children, a girl and a boy, play in the sunshine. The children are busy making mud pies, and their laughter reassures the man and woman that their children are content entertaining themselves. As the couple look away from their children, they return to a conversation about plans for a forthcoming holiday. There are flight reservations and hotel bookings to be made; discussing these plans, the woman makes notes about the intended weeks away from the routines of family life, commenting that she must check with her parents to see that they can look after the children. Their conversation is briefly disturbed when a call is taken on a mobile telephone; it is a business matter, and the man quickly switches from his previous conversation to the world of finance. Meanwhile, the woman briefly glances across at her children; reassuring herself that all is well, she returns to making plans for the holiday.

This might well be regarded as a typical scene in the life of an economically secure family in contemporary Western society. But what is going on here at the level of social interaction? In particular, what might this episode have to tell us about the nature of the self? The study of the minutiae of social interaction in everyday life is treated as of major importance by many sociologists, in part because it is at the level of human interaction and interpersonal relationships that the fabrication of the self arises. There are several traditions of sociological thought that study the self in the context of social interaction and daily life, and these traditions can be used to develop interesting interpretations of self, society and their mutual interaction. In the situation of the family sketched in the foregoing paragraph, we might, for example, focus on what sociologists term the 'contexts' of conversations and encounters navigated by the self. This would mean looking in some detail at how the man and woman make the necessary shifts in conversational positions between their own private talk, the practical accomplishment of maintaining this conversation while monitoring the activities of their children, and the suspension of their interpersonal conversation to engage with another style of talk altogether – in this case, that of business. Alternatively, we might instead concentrate on the children rather than the adults, giving special emphasis to their play. Some sociologists argue that, in children's play, we can detect the imitating of adult actions, and thus experimentation with different forms of self. In the making of mud pies, for instance, these children are most likely enacting their observations of adult cooking; the boy and girl might play at being father and mother, or chef and waitress. In effect, through such play-acting, these children are experimenting with different ways of being a self. Or perhaps we might look at this situation from another perspective, focusing on how a sense of self is sustained through institutional, and perhaps global, processes. Planning a holiday to some far-away country with ease, or the reception of an overseas phone call through new communications technology: here the self is seen as interacting with social forces that are global in scope.

We will look in this chapter at several different sociological approaches to the self and self-identity. In the first part of the chapter we will concentrate on the symbolic dimensions of social interaction and daily life, with particular emphasis on the importance of language, communication and symbols in the constitution of the self. The theoretical tradition of symbolic interactionism will be introduced, and the writings of G. H. Mead and Herbert Blumer will be discussed. We will then move on to analyse the importance of different forms of social interaction in everyday life for studying the self, and the work of the American sociologist Erving Goffman will be considered. After this we shall consider more recent developments in sociological theory that connect self and society in the context of global institutional processes, giving particular attention to the writings of the British sociologist Anthony Giddens.

Self, Symbols and Others: Symbolic Interactionism

We often think of the self as primarily a private domain, an inner realm of personal thoughts, values, strivings, emotions and desires. Yet this view, which seems largely self-evident, is in contrast to the way in which sociologists study the framing of personal identity and the self. Sociology demonstrates the need to look at the impact of other people, the wider society, as well as cultural forms and moral norms, in the making of the self. Particularly for sociologists interested in the dynamics of interpersonal interaction, the self can be thought of as a central mechanism through which the individual and the social world intersect. As such, the self, along with the attendant interpretations and definitions of situation and context that individuals routinely make in daily life, must be fully taken into account for the purposes of social analysis.

George Herbert Mead (1863–1931) is widely considered the founding father of a general tradition of theoretical thinking concerned with the self: symbolic interactionism. Interestingly, Mead did not refer to himself as a symbolic interactionist; he more typically thought of himself as a philosopher or social psychologist, and spent most of his professional life teaching at the University of Chicago. Mead's theoretical influences were wide-ranging. He had immersed himself in continental philosophy, as well as the developing American pragmatic tradition that included sociologists, psychologists and philosophers such as Charles H. Cooley (1864–1929), William I. Thomas (1863–1947), Charles S. Peirce (1839–1914), William James (1842–1910) and John Dewey (1859–1952). He drew liberally from these various authors to develop a powerful account of the emergence of a sense of self. While this in itself might sound a little daunting, it should be noted that Mead elaborated his theory of the self in a very clear style; hence his key ideas about the self can be set out without too much difficulty.

In *Mind, Self and Society* (Chicago: University of Chicago Press, 1934 [1974]), published after his death and constructed from the lecture notes of his students, Mead develops an interpretation of the social nature of the constitution of self. Broadly speaking, he places great emphasis upon the social self; each of us, as individuals, fashions a sense of our own selfhood through engagement with other selves. No clear dividing line can be drawn between our own sense of self and the selves of others, according to Mead, 'since our own selves exist and enter as such into our experience only in so far as the selves of others exist and enter as such into our experience also' (p. 164).

According to Mead, language is at the heart of the constitution of the self. Human beings, unlike the lower animals, communicate through symbols – hence the subsequent use of the term 'symbolic interaction'. Symbols represent objects in our own minds and in the minds of others; when we learn, in childhood, to think of an object symbolically – whether the object is a parent, sibling or doll – we are making an initial step on the road to reflective thinking and autonomous agency. Language is pivotal in this connection. Without access to language there is no access to the symbols necessary for thinking and acting as a self in a structured world of symbolic meaning. Symbols, says Mead, have a universal quality for the social groups in which they are meaningful; symbols are a common currency through which individuals forge a sense of self and interact with other people. There is thus a certain commonality to being a self, which means that, by looking at our own thoughts, feelings and attitudes, we can interpret the actions of others. To take the attitude of another is, in a sense, to identify with the other's viewpoint, position or feelings. A death in the family of a friend, for instance, will elicit feelings of sadness and sympathy, as we try to 'look at' our friend's situation by imagining how we might feel. We feel we know, almost exactly, the way that our friend feels, and the different ways he or she might react, partly because we try to imagine ourselves 'in their shoes'. The poet, Mead points out, relies on such commonalities when creating a pattern of words to evoke in others an experience of intense emotion.

The self for Mead is at once individuality and generality, agent and recipient, sameness and difference. Bluntly put, what this means is that the self is the agency through which individuals experience themselves in relation to others, but also an object or fact dealt with by its individual owner as he or she sees fit. We routinely construct our experience of daily life in exactly this manner: prodding, pushing, suggesting, advising, admonishing, criticizing and praising as we create the flow of our actions in the social world. 'Well done!', or just as easily 'you idiot!', we might say to ourselves when surveying the results of our actions; the crucial point for Mead is that such surveying of the territory of the self is always carried out with reference to the reactions of others. To possess a 'self' then necessarily implies an ability to take one's actions, emotions and beliefs as a unified structure, viewed from the perspective of significant others, as others would view and interpret actions of the self. Seen from this angle, the self is a social product through and through, an outcome of social symbolic interaction – of emergent, ongoing creation, thinking, feeling, the building of attitude structures, the taking on of roles, all in a quest for coherence and orientated to the social world.

Anyone who reflects on the dynamics of conversation and dialogue will know that ideas, attitudes, dispositions, tacit understandings and emotions cross and tangle between discussants, such that we manage to take away from a 'good conversation' something of the other person's concrete understanding of his or her identity and relationship to others, as well as the wider world. This is what Mead was driving at when he commented that the individual self is peopled with 'the attitude of others'. Across the entire spectrum of social life, we learn to view ourselves as other people see us, adjusting and transforming our self-understanding in the light of ongoing social interaction and dialogue. This ongoing dialogue between the self and others is what Mead termed 'the conversation of gestures', involving the exchange of symbols and the monitoring of interpretation and definition in all interaction. Social interaction is organized around such conversational gestures, as the individual travels along a bio-graphical trajectory from a preliminary or rudimentary sense of self in childhood to an adult identity, one geared to the values and moral dispositions of culture.

Child development in particular is central to Mead's under-standing of the self. Mead places considerable emphasis on the play of infants and young children in conceptualizing the emergence of a sense of self. For it is through play, he notes, that the small child learns about the social world and about interacting with it. Play tends to be at once rebellious and structured. It is rebellious in the sense that it drifts without apparent structure or order, especially among very young children. It is structured in the sense that the child adopts a series of symbolically defined social roles. Consider, once more, the boy and girl playing in the garden as their parents look on. In the making of mud pies, the boy and girl might be trying on the hats of father and mother one moment, and then shopkeeper and customer the next; in doing so, the children have all the attitudes and responses, more or less adequately defined, worked out. The boy and girl are able to manipulate a series of characters, imitating what they have seen their parents do, or similarly what they have seen actors do on television. This is what Mead termed 'taking the role of the other', a key way in which the self becomes attuned to the demands and pressures of society. In fact, Mead thought that, in the play of children, one could glimpse the rudiments of a differentiated social order: different roles interact, com-plement and reciprocate responsibilities and duties. And this pattern becomes part of the self.

I said before that the self from the perspective of symbolic interactionism is a social product, but this now needs to be qualified somewhat. Mead makes a crucial distinction between the 'I' and the 'me' in conceptualizing the self. The 'me' is the socialized self, made up of the internalized attitudes of others as experienced in the early years of life. The 'I', as Mead uses the term, is the unsocialized self, an assortment of personal desires, needs and dispositions. These more spontaneous wants and wishes of the 'I' serve to distinguish the self from others, and can be said to inject something new, creative and innovative into the social process. The achievement of self-awareness, says Mead, arises when the self is able to distinguish the 'me' from the 'I', and hence attain a level of reflective distance from the demands of society and culture. This conceptual move also allows Mead to avoid the charge that his theory of the self is deterministic – that is, that the self is a mere reflection of the attitudes of general society, or an internalization of social structure. Mead's theory of the self is at some considerable distance from such determinism, since he holds that each individual responds to social relations in a particularistic or unique fashion. 'The attitudes involved', he writes (1974, p. 198), 'are gathered from the group, but the individual in whom they are organized has the opportunity of giving them an expression which perhaps has never taken place before.' Mead's distinction between 'me' and 'I' thus introduces a level of contingency and ambivalence to each social encounter: the 'I' reacts to the 'me' in a social context, but we cannot be sure exactly how that 'I' will react. Accordingly, the 'I' in interaction with the 'me' plays a role in the transformation of social structure.

Another significant figure in symbolic interactionism is Herbert Blumer (1900–87). A pupil of Mead, Blumer sought to explicate the implications of Mead's theories for the analysis of the self in the social sciences. Blumer argued that what was peculiar to the social sciences was that human agents interpret and define their own action, as well as the action of others, instead of merely reacting to human behaviour in a mechanical fashion. This meant that those sociologists (and there were many at the time) who believed that the objectives and logic of social science were the same as those of natural science were in error; the study of human conduct is, in fact, considerably different from the analysis of the movement of objects and events in nature. According to Blumer, a naturalistic perspective in social science can have no proper grasp of the distinctive symbolic qualities of the self. Human interaction, says Blumer, is 'mediated by the use of symbols, by interpretation, or by ascertaining the meaning of one another's actions' (Herbert Blumer, 'Society as Symbolic Interaction' in A. Rose (ed.), *Human Behaviour and Social Process*, London: Routledge and Kegan Paul, 1962, p. 180). To raise the issue of interpretation here is to question the process by which selves attach meaning to human experience. Objects, according to Blumer, are not simply stimuli for action; they are rather perceived through a process of 'making indications to the self' (ibid.: 181). Conscious life, the life of the self, is an ongoing process of self-indication. What this means, in effect, is that everything perceived in social life refers back to the self, and is given meaning by self-interpretation. Individual action, says Blumer, is thus 'a construction and not a release' (ibid.: 184), developed in an ongoing process through constant monitoring and interpretation of self-indications, of what others are intending and doing, of the roles they are taking on, and the like.

For symbolic interactionists, therefore, the study of social life is closely interwoven with the analysis of the meaning of human action that individuals actively construct and interpret. Such an understanding of the creative involvement of the self has led to a sensitivity, on the part of some sociologists, to the complexity of social interaction – to the context in which individuals communicate, including the interpretations such individuals have of that context, and of the identities of those involved. Sociological interactionists pay close attention to the explanations, tacit understandings and meanings that individuals give to their own actions, as well as to the actions of others.

However, symbolic interactionism has several weaknesses, which limits its attraction as a general theoretical framework for the study of the self. One major criticism is that the model of the self outlined by Mead and his followers is too rationalistic, conscious and cognitive. For many critics, the self painted by symbolic interactionists is primarily a matter of thinking, not of emotion or passion. Now Mead tended to associate 'feeling' with the physiological realm, a realm that he separated off from the self. Accordingly, his account of the self sometimes appears as peculiarly disembodied, something that many influenced by the writings of recent feminists and postmodernists would consider inadequate for developing a critical theory of the self.

Similarly, the emphasis on the cognitive at the expense of the emotional realm in symbolic interactionism has been criticized as inadequate by authors influenced by the insights of Freud into unconscious elements of motivation of the self. The self for Freud, as we will see in the next chapter, is structured by unconscious promptings – desires, wishes, fantasies. By contrast, Mead's theory of the self does not rely on a theory of unconscious forces at the centre of mind and the self. The self is seen as primarily cognitive by symbolic interactionists because the seeds of self-consciousness are understood to derive from individuals consciously manipulating and constructing identity in accordance with that 'conversation of gestures' established through engagement with the social process. From a Freudian standpoint, however, Mead and his followers set up a conception of the relationship between self and society that is too smooth. As the self is constructed entirely through interaction – the individual looking at the self, as it were, as others see him or her – there would seem to be little or no conflict between the individual and society. There is no recognition of the tension, say, that Freud referred to in books like *Civilization and its Discontents*: between individual desires, wishes and fantasies on the one hand, and the requirements for social control and cultural order on the other. Mead claims that access to language permits us to become self-conscious agents, reproducing the values and morality of society through our developed capacity for self-awareness and self-understanding. However, there is no sense of the slippage or tension in Mead's vision between self-consciousness and other levels of experience, including bodily experience and unconscious forms of thought.

Finally, symbolic interactionism has difficulty assessing more political issues concerning the self and self-identity, such as the complex ways in which processes of cultural exclusion work to harm and damage the development of the self. Mead argued that the issue of social control was not in fact problematic for the individual because of the manner in which the demands of society entered into the construction of the self. As Mead develops this, 'self-criticism is essentially social criticism, and behaviour controlled by self-criticism is essentially behaviour controlled socially. Hence social control, so far from tending to crush out the human individual or to obliterate his self-conscious individuality, is, on the contrary, actually constitutive of and inextricably associated with that individuality.' Taken too far, however, this viewpoint might occlude any conception of political domination. The writings of the French historian Michel Foucault, whose work is discussed in chapter 3, presents, by contrast, a far less benign view of the social fabrication of the individual self in relation to the social network. For social theorists influenced by Foucault, or indeed by his contemporary, the French psycho-analyst Jacques Lacan, the structured world of social interaction can be far more crushing of individual expression than that which is acknowledged in the perspective of symbolic interactionism.

Yet if symbolic interactionists never quite spell out the various forms in which social and political relations of power and domination enter into the construction of the self, it remains the case that this general theoretical framework high-lights the extremely subtle process by which symbolic inter-pretation shapes identities and defines the interaction between self and others in the course of day-to-day social life. At its best, Mead's work underscores certain themes that have come to be very important to contemporary discussions about the self: children develop a sense of identity through active, creative engagement with others and the wider world; language and communication are pivotal to the fabrication of personal identity and the self; and the development of self-consciousness is intimately interwoven with taking on the role of others.

Presentations of Self: Goffman

Erving Goffman (1922–82) is widely considered one of the most brilliant and innovative sociological observers of daily life, social interaction and the production of self. He analyses our day-to-day activities with reference to the metaphor of the theatre, looking at what is most common and habitual in the ways that individuals perform roles and stage-manage impressions within specific social settings. The self consists for Goffman in an awareness of the multiplicity of roles that are performed in various situated contexts; such performances involve individuals in continually monitoring the impressions they give off to, and make upon, others; public identity is thus performed for an audience, and the private self knows that such performances are essential to identity and to the maintenance of respect and trust in routine social interaction.

One might suppose, from these introductory remarks, that Goffman develops a sociological overview of the socially constructed self. This is partly accurate, as Goffman emphasizes the importance of symbolically defined roles, statuses and relationships that individuals engage with in creating impressions of the self for others – and to this extent his work reflects the imprint of the tradition of symbolic interactionism. (Goffman undertook his graduate studies at the University of Chicago in the 1940s, where he came under the influence of Herbert Blumer). Yet, although Goffman is sometimes portrayed as a symbolic interactionist, his work in fact conceptualizes the self in exactly the sense that symbolic interactionism does not consider – that is, the individual is viewed by Goffman as at once drawing from and transcending specific roles and norms in the strategic manipulation of impressions in everyday life. In other words, identity might be constructed through the adoption of, and adherence to, social roles and their validation by social institutions, but the individual is the creative and reflective agent who decides – and in doing so constitutes self-identity – on how to carry out such roles as well as the staging of role performances.

In his most celebrated book, *The Presentation of Self in Everyday Life* (1956), Goffman analyses with great wit and verve the routine or taken-for-granted details of face-to-face interaction. His central preoccupation is with the dramatic techniques by which the self displays agency to others. Dismantling conventional assumptions that equate selfhood with inner character or personality, Goffman writes:

> [The self] does not derive from its possessor, but from the whole scene of his action, being generated by that attribute of local events which renders them interpretable by witnesses. A correctly staged and performed scene leads the audience to impute a self to the performed character, but this imputation – this self – is a *product* of a scene that comes off, and is not a *cause* of it. The self, then, as a performed character, is not an organic thing that has a specific location, whose fundamental fate is to be born, to mature, and to die; it is a dramatic effect arising diffusely from a scene that is presented, and the

characteristic issue, the crucial concern, is whether it will be credited or discredited. (*The Goffman Reader*, ed. C. Lemert and A. Branaman, Oxford: Blackwell, 1997, pp. 23–4)

To speak of identity as a 'dramatic effect' is, in short, to dismantle the customary equation of self and mind. If identity is performed, then the self is an effect, not a cause. We might tend to think of the self as the source of our activities, ideas, beliefs or ways of being in the world, but in fact we retroactively attribute private intentions and subjective capabilities to our identities through the realization of skilled social performance.

Consider, for example, what Goffman terms 'role distance'. Role distance is conceptualized by Goffman as the means whereby an individual expresses a separation between role and self. Thus the university student who works as a shop assistant during the summer holidays is not symbolically defined by this social role because of the social meanings attributed to being a student and the status of holiday work. In drawing attention to the separation of role and self, however, Goffman does not suggest that identity is concealed behind roles, or that performers can be seen in a more accurate light as standing behind their performance. On the contrary, role distance allows an opportunity for the individual self to constitute himself or herself with due seriousness and credibility. Hence, a doctor who engages in some small talk with patients might be able to lessen the anxieties of patients about the medical consultation and thereby provide reassurance as to his or her medical competence. In this sense, role distance can promote the professional credibility of the self.

We can draw out the intimate connections between productions of self and contexts of interaction, according to Goffman, by looking closely at the 'face' or 'façade' that individuals seek to achieve in the stylization of their conduct and behaviour with others. All presentations of self, says Goffman, are situated within interactive frameworks involving social conventions, ethical assumptions and the positioning of bodies in relation to the physical features of settings. In seeking to present a self-image that is acceptable within any given interactive framework, individuals must necessarily come to make certain distinctions between what Goffman calls 'front' and 'back' regions. The frontal aspects of self-presentation routinely involve the bracketing-out or screening-off of aspects of identity which are felt to be inappropriate to the social setting or encounter that is staged. Thus, the 'face' of authority that a television newsreader seeks to present (using the dress props of a jacket and tie) may contrast significantly with the jeans he is wearing, but which cannot be seen on screen. In most areas of social life the 'upfront' performances of individuals contrast with back-region behaviour, where individuals do not have to worry so much about the face they seek to project. In some sectors of social life – for example, in restaurants – the distinction between front and back regions is reasonably well defined and fixed. But the use of regional demarcations is essential, in Goffman's view, to the contextuality of all human interaction and dramatization of self.

Goffman argues that the individual must continually display competence of self to others and to the social world. This involves the chronic monitoring of self-identity. But it also goes further, involving a kind of watchfulness over the most seemingly trivial aspects of social behaviour – including the control of bodily management. Goffman describes one category of our attempts to remedy lapses in self-watchfulness as 'response cries': 'A woman rapidly walking to a museum exit, passes the door, catches her mistake, utters *Oops!*, and backtracks to the right place' (ibid., p. 193). The woman's response cry (‘*Oops!*’) might at first sight appear impulsive, expressive or unsocialized; her blurted cry, after all, does not seem to be directed at another. Not so, says Goffman. In uttering such a protective-like cry, he suggests, the woman demonstrates to others around her some presence of mind, indicating an awareness of her incompetence, and thus confirming for others that it was only a lapse. We employ response cries to demonstrate self-monitoring and self-control to others; 'response cries', says Goffman, 'do not mark a flooding of emotion outward, but a flooding of relevance in' (ibid., p. 196).

Goffman's work, as we have seen, tends to concentrate on the maintenance and manipulation of the self: the theoretical questions it asks stem from the individual's management of impressions, performed in the unending social situations of everyday life. Not all the emphasis of this approach, however, is on the creative fashioning of self. Goffman is in fact careful to guard against an overly idealistic vision of the social construction of self, a vision that some critics nonetheless believe his theory promotes – as we will examine shortly. To avoid reducing the self to random acts of identity invention in which the individual appears unencumbered by social mores, Goffman also concentrates on certain constraining aspects which shape the self and which govern the personal responses of individuals. In his classic collection of essays, *Asylums* (1961), Goffman looks at the disruption, and oftentimes dispossession, of the self that arises when individuals live under abnormal constraints in institutions such as mental hospitals, prisons and detention camps. *Asylums* was Goffman's account of the daily life of psychiatric inmates at a hospital in the United States during the late 1950s. From his close personal observations of life in a psychiatric hospital, he formulated his influential notion of 'total institution': an institution is total, for example, when it imposes regulations on most aspects of the lives of individuals, in everything from eating and sleeping to work and relaxation. Total institutions such as asylums and prisons, says Goffman, are 'forcing houses for changing persons; each is a natural experiment on what can be done to the self' (Erving Goffman, Asylums, NY: Anchor Books, 1961, p.12). We have now moved from the self of performance to the self of programming.

Goffman identifies various processes by which an individual's sense of self is programmed in degrading or stigmatized ways under the abnormal conditions of total institutions. Reporting on what he calls 'the moral career of the mental patient', he describes in minute detail the complex strategies through which hospitals come to impose degrading routines, humiliating rituals and deference patterns to figures of authority upon patients:

> Like the neophyte in many of these total institutions, the new impatient finds himself cleanly stripped of many of his accustomed affirmations, satisfactions, and defenses, and is subject to a rather full set of mortifying experiences: restriction of free movement, communal living, diffuse authority of a whole

echelon of people, and so on. Here one begins to learn about the limited extent to which a conception of oneself can be sustained when the usual setting of supports for it are suddenly removed. (Goffman, *Asylums*, p.148)

From ignoring forms of tact that would normally be found in the rest of society to submitting inmates to strip searches and other humiliating circumstances, Goffman detects here the gradual but steady erosion of an individual's normal sense of self. As he says, total institutions produce a 'mortification of self'. By screening out the rest of the world, psychiatric and carceral organizations enclose individuals within a restricted, identity-trimming milieu. But more than this, the mortification of self imposed by total institutions contrasts powerfully with the relative freedom that people enjoy in the rest of society. As such, the study of total institutions tells us a great deal about the necessary social processes that underpin ordinary presentations of self in public.

There is a certain magic that comes from reading Goffman's disturbing guides to territories of the self. In fact, the social world may never seem quite the same after you read him: what appeared as simply natural or taken-for-granted is catapulted into layers of complex, hidden social processes which constitute self-identity to its core. That said, however, Goffman's theory of the self is not without its difficulties. To begin with, there is something a little disturbing in his social vision of performance, in which everyone is cynically manipulating appearance and staging inauthentic representations of the self. Such is the view, at any rate, of the American sociologist Alvin Gouldner, who argues in a celebrated critique that Goffman presents us with an amoral social universe. For Gouldner, Goffman's work is expressive of some of the most insidious ideological aspects of American mass culture, a culture in which marketing, manipulation and media reach all the way down to the textures of personal identity and the self. One way of grasping this criticism might be to frame Goffman's performing self in the image of Woody Allen's oddest character, Leonard Zelig, a man so lacking in selfhood that his life completely dissolves into role-playing. Zelig is focused to such a degree on making a good impression on others that he, literally, takes on the personality of whomever he is with – at one moment, in a jazz club, he becomes a black musician; at another moment, when eating spaghetti in a restaurant, he becomes Italian; later he turns up in Germany as a member of Hitler's Nazi party. Understanding Goffman's performing self in terms of Allen's movie *Zelig* is useful perhaps only up to a point, but it does offer us a grim sense of the psychological costs of impression management in a culture in which a premium is put on appearance.

While Goffman undoubtedly emphasizes the performative dimension of self-constitution, it is not altogether clear that he sees people as mere performers putting on a show or manipulating impressions. Indeed, Randall Collins argues that Goffman's sociology suggests precisely the opposite, with the self portrayed as moral through and through. According to Collins, people routinely engage in interactional rituals geared towards moral order, in which respect for others, social tact and interpersonal trust are expressed. From this angle, moral order is not the upshot of an internalization of ethical obligations – as with, say, Mead; rather, morality is part of the process of the production of the self. Morality is not just a set of external rules or prohibitions; it is, rather, a binding feature of the complex ways in which individuals achieve a consistent definition of their worlds in daily interaction.

Whether one concludes that there is or is not a moral sensibility at the heart of Goffman's account of skilled social performances, it remains perhaps hard to see why the performing self might in any event be worried or anxious about impression management – for Goffman's theory of self says surprisingly little about the emotional or psychosexual dynamics of personal life and social relationships. Goffman, to be sure, maintained that there is a self standing behind the multitude of roles that any individual performs in daily social interaction; the problem, however, is that he is very vague on the psychic orientations or emotional dispositions that shape the acting self. A psychoanalytical interpretation of his performative self, for example, might view such undue concern with impression management as symptomatic of deeper anxieties of the self – anxieties stirred perhaps by narcissism, and damaging to the individual's sense of self-worth and autonomy. It is not easy to see how Goffman's theory of self could be used to analyse such disturbances of personal identity.

Questions of desire, then, do not enter into Goffman's reflections on the self; but the image of the self as situated performer surely also throws into doubt the emphasis on a 'true self' that modern culture valorizes, and which is evident in many forms of social thought – including some versions of psychoanalytical theory. In debunking the idea that the self is stabilized according to the internalization of moral norms and cultural ideals, Goffman transforms the way in which individual subjectivity is conceived. This involves a shift from seeing the self as outcome (a product of, say, family, society or history) to a more fluid conception of the self as situationally defined. Much social theory, in particular postmodern theory, is devoted to a view of personal identity and social life as filtered through surfaces, images, performances, fragments and constructions. Goffman's theory of the performative self might well be understood as a precursor to such postmodernist sensibilities.

Reflexivity and the Self: Giddens

The influence of Anthony Giddens's work in sociology is comparable to that of Goffman. Both have developed powerful interpretations of the self. Yet while Goffman developed his theory of the self on the basis of observations drawn from interpersonal interaction, Giddens ties his account of the self much more to institutional and global forces. Giddens (b. 1938) spent the greater part of his academic career at Cambridge University, and subsequently became Director of the London School of Economics. He has written an extraordinary number of books – on social theory, philosophy, politics and the history of sociological thought. In the 1990s he became increasingly preoccupied with the role of the self in social analysis, and his books *Modernity and Self-Identity* (1991) and *The Transformation of Intimacy* (1992) have strongly influenced debates in social theory.

At the core of Giddens's theory of the self is the concept of 'reflexivity', a concept of immense significance for grasping the production of personal and social life. Reflexivity can be defined as a self-defining process that depends upon monitoring of, and reflection upon, psychological and social information about possible trajectories of life. Such information about self and world is not simply incidental to contemporary cultural life; it is actually constitutive of what people do and how they do it. 'The reflexivity of modern social life', writes Giddens, 'consists in the fact that social practices are constantly examined and reformed in the light of incoming information about those very practices, thus constitutively altering their character' (Anthony Giddens, *The Consequences of Modernity*, Cambridge: Polity, p. 38). In one sense, what is underscored here concerns the richness of the sense-making process, primarily the mixings of certainty and anxiety that allow an individual to *read* cultural life and its textured flow of social action. This imperative to read cultural signs with some degree of sophistication is perhaps an index of our postmodern, speed-driven information age, evident in everything from serious social criticism (in which commentary refers to previous commentary, which in turn is premised upon prior commentary) to the latest trends in pop music, which routinely invoke parodies of style and genre. In another sense, reflexivity stretches beyond the cultural and subjective, deeply rooted as it is in institutional social life. From mapping the demographic characteristics of cities to monitoring the changing flight paths of aircraft, the intrusion of expert reflexive systems into daily life is pivotal to the world of modernity.

Consider, for example, the connections between marriage, the family and self-identity. There are few areas of social life that more directly affect the self than that of marriage and the family. Traditionally, the marriage tie was primarily structured as an economic arrangement: the husband used the marriage as a place from which to organize his activities in the public world, while the wife concentrated on children and the home. The idea of romantic love significantly weakened the power of such economic considerations, although marriage as an institution within patriarchy has undoubtedly remained intimately interwoven with economic power. Marriage of the late modern type, in Western societies at any rate, has provided an institutional context in which men and women can pursue the achievement of intimacy, respect, love, equality, autonomy and self-integrity. Notwithstanding changes in the relationship between the sexes in recent decades, the notion of romantic love remains psychologically central to the pursuit of personal and sexual fulfilment within marriage. Alongside this, marriage has been a key arena for the psychic development of the self, as this is organized through attitudes associated with childhood, adolescence and the nurturing of intimate sentiments within general social relations.

However, these days, 'till-death-us-do-part' marriages seem the product of a bygone age. In many of the advanced societies, nearly half of first marriages end in divorce, and the statistics are worse for second and subsequent marriages. But what are the broader cultural consequences of our separating and divorcing society? What impact are divorce, remarriage and the rise of de facto relationships having at the level of personal experience and the self? How is the texture of individuals' personal lives altered by the disintegration of family ties that bind? For conservative social critics, marriage break-up is perhaps the key sign of society's moral decay. In this critique the weakening of marriage as an institution is related to sexual permissiveness, as well as a moral deficiency, which the decline of the patriarchal family has created. A number of long-term social influences are usually identified in this connection, including the sexual revolution of the 1960s, the rise of feminism, the spread of alternative lifestyles, pornography and the drug culture.

Under the impact of these social forces, according to conservatives, the self withdraws from public life and political obligation, moral bonds recede in favour of an overwhelming desire for instant narcissistic gratification, and intimate relationships fragment into short-term, provisional and episodic encounters.

Yet this view, which has gained considerable currency in the political sphere in recent times, is in fact premised upon a defensive rejection of the actual responses of people to the complex, contradictory experience of divorce and remarriage. In the conservative critique, individuals appear as largely passive in their reactions to transformations in intimacy affecting self and culture. Against this backdrop, individuals

cannot help but appear shut out from an emotionally reward-
ing and satisfying life. But it is simply not the case that
individuals passively equate the end of marriage with the
disintegration of self; nor is it the case that people give up
hope of refashioning their identity and sense of well-being.

This is where Giddens enters the debate, bringing his
account of reflexivity to bear on marriage, divorce and the
self. According to him, individuals today actively engage with
fresh opportunities and dangers that arise as a consequence
of dramatic and shattering transformations affecting
self-identity, sexuality and intimacy. For Giddens, divorce is
undeniably a crisis for the self, involving significant pain, loss
and mourning. Yet many people, he argues, take positive
steps to work through the emotional dilemmas generated by
marriage breakdown; in addition to dealing with financial
issues and matters affecting how children should be brought
up, separation and divorce also call into play an emotional
engagement with the self. Charting territory of the past (where
things went wrong, missed opportunities, etc.) and of the
future (alternative possibilities, chances for self-actualization,
etc.) necessarily involves experimenting with a new sense of
self. This can lead to emotional growth, new understandings
of self, and strengthened intimacies. Against the conservative
critique of irredeemable breakdown, Giddens sees the self
opening out to constructive renewal. Remarriage and the
changing nature of family life are crucial in this regard for
Giddens. As he develops this point:

> Many people, adults and children, now live in stepfamilies –
> not usually, as in previous eras, as a consequence of the death
> of a spouse, but because of the re-forming of marriage ties
> after divorce. A child in a stepfamily may have two mothers
> and fathers, two sets of brothers and sisters, together with
> other complex kin connections resulting from the multiple
> marriages of parents. Even the terminology is difficult: should
> a stepmother be called 'mother' by the child, or called by her
> name? Negotiating such problems might be arduous and psy-
> chologically costly for all parties; yet opportunities for novel
> kinds of fulfilling social relations plainly also exist. One thing
> we can be sure of is that the changes involved here are not
> just external to the individual. These new forms of extended
> family ties have to be established by the very persons who find

themselves most directly caught up in them. (Anthony Giddens, *Modernity and Self-Identity*, Cambridge: Polity, 1991, p. 13)

Marital separation, as portrayed by Giddens, implicates the self in an open project: tracing over the past, imagining the future, dealing with complex family problems and experimenting with a new sense of identity. Further experimentation with marriage and intimate relationships will necessarily involve anxieties, risks and opportunities. But, as Giddens emphasizes, the relation between self and society is a highly fluid one, involving negotiation, change and development.

The manner in which current social practices shape future life outcomes is nowhere more in evidence than in the conjunction of divorce statistics, the reckoning of probability ratios for success or failure in intimate relationships, and the decision to get married. As Giddens rightly points out, statistics about marriage and divorce do not exist in a social vacuum; everyone, he says, is in some sense aware of how present gender uncertainties affect long-term relationships. When people marry or remarry today, according to Giddens, they do so against a cultural backdrop of high divorce statistics, knowledge of which alters a person's understanding and conception of what marriage actually is. It is precisely this reflexive monitoring of relationships that, in turn, transforms expectations about, and aspirations for, marriage and intimacy. The relationship between self, society and reflexivity is a dynamic one, involving the continual overturning of traditional ways of doing things.

Despite the influence and interest of Giddens's work for many social theorists, others have responded with bemusement and disbelief to his claim that the self is a self-mastering, self-monitoring project. For Giddens's critics, the reflexive project of self-making and self-actualization exhibits a distinctively individualistic bent, in a social theory that reduces struggle over power and politics to mere personal interest in change. The core concern here is that Giddens's theory of the reflexive self fits too neatly with the liberal ideology of individualism – the notion that the sovereign individual self lies at the heart of society. My own view is that such criticism is somewhat misplaced, since Giddens is at pains to underscore the increasing interconnection between personal life and globalizing social influences. The reflexive self is not then so much self-mastering (though Giddens sometimes implies as much) as reflexively implicated in the thrills and spills of social life. Yet there is a difficulty with the almost excessive emphasis that Giddens places on the tacit knowledge and self-understanding of social agents – excessive since it threatens to break the link with issues of social power and political domination that he recognizes in his writings elsewhere. Particularly for social theorists and cultural critics influenced by post-structuralist and postmodern accounts of domination and powerlessness, the individual – through knowledge and experience of social practices, cultural codes and moral norms – can be critically analysed in terms of enacted restrictive performances or repressive forms of self-actualization. From this angle, what Giddens takes as a sign of reflexive agency is, in fact, a form of social control.

It would seem that Giddens's attempt to situate the self in terms of reflexive monitoring is also destined to clash with psychoanalytic constructions of subjectivity in terms of fantasy and repressed desire. Psychoanalytic critics, as will be discussed in the next chapter, have used a variety of strategies to connect Freudian thought to the current ambivalences and evasions of culture and politics. Of core importance in this connection is the multiplicity of unconscious ties and attachments as manifested in the self's relations with others; in contrast to traditional understandings of the individual as self-identical and rational, the individual is revealed in psychoanalysis to exhibit a range of subjective identifications available in fantasy. The notion of multiple subjective identifications, as experienced in unconscious fantasy, is potentially troubling to Giddens's self-monitoring reflexive self – primarily because it threatens a range of conceptual oppositions upon which his work rests, including active/passive, knowledge/desire, and mind/body.

This criticism can be made more concrete by returning to the example of intimacy and marriage. Women and men, we can agree with Giddens, pursue intimate relationships today against a cultural backdrop of dramatic transformations governing sexuality, love, marriage, the family and work. Many embrace these social changes wholeheartedly; others may have mixed impressions; some no doubt try to carry on by ignoring current shifts in gender thinking and practice. Yet these social and sexual issues undoubtedly press in on everyone as personal matters and interpersonal crises. Giddens is surely right, then, to tie self and society ineluctably together around our reflexive discontents over sexuality and gender. But however aware of the current historical moment we may try to be, we are all linked to specific emotional pasts and prior generational histories – and this is where Giddens's work runs into difficulties, as he seems to downplay the degree to which the influence of emotion, memory and desire can limit or conflict with our conscious attempts to order our lives and make sense of the world in more reflexive terms. Thus a person who has suffered emotional abandonment by a parent in childhood might display a quite defensive emotional need to embrace, or equally to deny, intimacy; such needs and desires, while not automatically in conflict with reflexive knowledge of the self and world, do not reduce to the language of social practices.

I began this book by questioning the idea that the self is more a psychological than a social, or even political, concept. I also argued that individual subjectivity, far from being an agency through which the self sustains and reproduces identity, might be more a product of how the individual internalizes, and responds in the process to, the obligations of culture and the demands of social life. Now we can see that how individuals form conceptions of identity is a central problem for any sociology. To emphasize the impact of social forms and cultural traditions on the self is not to imply that the individual is merely the product of external forces. On the contrary, the cultural resources and socio-symbolic materials from which individuals draw in the construction of personal experience and identity are always creatively engaged with, interpreted and transformed in the process of being reproduced. This emerges very clearly from Mead's account of the social origins of the self. According to Mead, the self is a symbolic project which the individual actively constructs and develops, drawing on symbolic resources to construct a sense of identity in the context of engagement with familial figures and the 'generalized other'. Symbolic interaction of this sort, upon which the making and remaking of the self depends, is not removed from the material conditions of daily life or the cultural forces that influence social interaction. The capacity to engage with the self and with others in contexts of socio-symbolic interaction is anchored in the routine, practical situations of day-to-day life. We have seen some of the problems that Mead's sociology of the self encounters in trying to relate these aspects of individual self-construction to socio-symbolic forms of interaction. Part of the problem, I have suggested, arises from Mead's failure to develop a conception of social differentiation, as well as his failure to account for processes of personal and social transformation.

That the self is a *knowledgeable agent* emerges clearly from the work of Mead and other symbolic interactionists. However, as Goffman's work shows, knowledgeability of self is fundamentally tied to the thousands of small interpersonal settings in and through which day-to-day life is organized. Thus individuals routinely 'repair' or 'shore up' the self through engaging in 'remedial practices'; by helping others to save face; and, above all, through the monitoring and manipulation of appearances in focused interaction. Most of us recognize, most of the time, that appearances are fundamental in our dealings with others that we come upon. Goffman's theory of the self provides a detailed conceptual account of why this should be so, although many critics have argued that the self is reduced in his work to the level of cynical manipulator of appearances. I have suggested that Goffman's account of the self is considerably more complex than such criticism seems to acknowledge; trust and tact are binding features of social interaction, and hence crucial to the constitution and reproduction of personal identity. It is, in fact, arguable that Goffman's theory of the self describes a highly moralized world of social relationships; his work shows that morality enters into the most practical accomplishments of the self.

Some contemporary critics are likely to be worried by the problem of the relationship between the individual self and social interaction, or between identity and social structure. In the account I sketched of Giddens's sociology of self-identity, I tried to show that there is a great deal more at stake here than the way in which personal identity is structured by existing social relations. For the self, according to Giddens, should be conceived as a continuous process of reflexivity, in a world in which vast institutional transformations associated with modernity enter into the fabric of who we are and how we conceive of ourselves. In Giddens's sociology, the capability for autonomous thought and reflexivity permits a sort of emotional regrooving of self in the broader context of contemporary social transformations sweeping the globe. Here Giddens has in mind the current phase of globalization transforming modern societies, particularly in the areas of politics, economics, culture and communication, migration, environmental issues, public policy and military affairs. By showing how complex processes of globalization are reshaping the self, Giddens's work highlights, in a sophisticated theoretical manner, the ways in which identity and social structure continually interweave. Critics of Giddens's account of the self divide between those who rather enthusiastically promote the reflexive orientations of identity in the late modern or postmodern age and those who insist, more pessimistically but perhaps more plausibly, that the reflexive capabilities of the self are overshadowed by various forces – including the system of social relations, of desire and of language.

What the various sociologies of the self that I have been charting fail to see is that identity also belongs to the peculiar kind of emotional needs that all of us experience and express in our personal and social worlds. By 'emotional needs' I refer not to something outside our social determination, but rather to the complex affective ways in which individual selves interact with others in the social world.

Twentieth-century sociological theory, as this chapter has suggested, provided a refined theoretical armoury to understand the constitution of the self. Yet sociologies of the self, however much they may explore the trajectories and transformations of intimacy and personal life, have scarcely shown much concern with the internal world of self-experience. Giddens seemed aware of this dilemma in his own way, and it is perhaps for this reason that he has sought to take the sociology of the self in a more personal or emotive direction. However, the century also provided other, somewhat darker, theoretical visions of the self, which we can now turn to examine.

2
The Repression of Self

At its simplest, the self can be thought of as mediator between mind and matter, the interweaving of our internal and external worlds. As the sociological approaches discussed in the previous chapter underscore, individuals develop a framework for defining the self in connection with the routines and flows of society and culture. In particular, experience of the self is strongly influenced by the actions and reactions of other people in day-to-day social life. Cognizance of the nature, depth and contours of interpersonal relationships is central to the constitution and reproduction of identity, as well as the embedding of selfhood in the context of social, cultural and political life. To reflect on this aspect of the self is to appreciate that identity is a *constructed* phenomenon. This means having an awareness that identity is established through individual actions and choices, the patterning of thoughts, dispositions, feelings and desires, and the structuring of subjective experience in relation to the social order. Most of us have some sense, however partial, that we perform or act out particular roles in our relationships with others; we have an awareness of the different sorts of identity we fashion when moving between the social settings of daily life. The ways in which an individual acts in the presence of family members or loved ones is likely to be rather different from encounters with, say, work colleagues or sporting partners. From family, school and work to shopping, community associations or surfing the Internet: all these social fields summon forth, and through them we construct, different sorts of self. Notwithstanding the myriad selves through which we experiment and define our experience in the wider world, it is not unusual for individuals to feel that there is something – some inner core of the self – that makes them whole. Rather than see the self as simply a private response to changing symbolic contexts, there remains for many people a sense of cohesive identity that presides over, and responds to, the social challenges and contexts of day-to-day life.

The issue of personal identity is highly contested in the social sciences and the humanities today, as the various chapters in this book demonstrate. There are those, for instance, who regard a core sense of self as central to the navigation of personal and public life; it is also sometimes held by theorists aligned with this position that the self is actively constructed through engagement with other people and the wider world. Yet others have argued that, however much an individual actively constructs her or his world, the fashioned self is continually bombarded with shifting cultural stimuli and fragmenting social phenomena. For such theorists it becomes more and more difficult to construct any unity for the self in a world in which social convulsion and ideological turmoil lurk beneath the surface of personal life and intimate relationships. Still others approach the troubles of selfhood less in terms of the complex conundrums thrown up by the political history of recent times than as a matter of psychic pleasure and its repression, and emotional gratification and its denial. The central focus in this standpoint concerns emotions, desires, wishes and impulses – in short, the inner world of the self. The relationship between self and society here is one of conflict, tension and ambivalence, but not simply because of impinging social or historical forces. Instead, emotional dislocation and sexual contradiction are treated as inherent to problems of the self. In this view, desire is at the root of the complex ways in which the individual and society interpenetrate. Problems of personal unhappiness and lack of fulfilment, of guilt and moral values, of sexual and gender troubles, of self-destructiveness and dissatisfaction, of aggression, destructiveness and violence: such forms of social and cultural estrangement are also fundamentally psychological.

That is to say, the organization of society penetrates to the emotional core of the lives of its members.

Such an understanding of selfhood, with its stress on how the individual fits into the social world only as troubled and troubling, is substantially indebted to the insights of the founder of psychoanalysis, Sigmund Freud. It is Freud, perhaps more than any other single figure, who has most influenced modern conceptions of the self. Yet any attempt to talk of Freud and his theories usually leads to various difficulties, because there are numerous versions of the master of psychoanalysis. There is Freud the founder of the unconscious mind, delighting in the riddles of self-knowledge and uncovering the cover-ups of repression. There is Freud the sexual radical, stressing the inherent contradictions of sexuality and gender identity, disdaining talk of 'normal' sexual relations, and proclaiming the 'perverse' origins of human sexuality. Equally, there is Freud the moralist, maintaining normative gender assumptions, and finding structure and order at the core of human relationships. There is Freud the champion of individual freedom, and Freud the social realist, who claimed there is no cure for unconscious desire. There is Freud the apostle of the Enlightenment, and even Freud the postmodernist, relentlessly declaring the incompleteness and insufficiency of human subjectivity. Everyone, it seems, has an opinion about Freud and the theoretical edifice of psychoanalysis. For those captivated by Freud's compelling insistence on sexual contradiction and emotional inconsistency, he is a genius. Others have argued that he was a charlatan, a bogus medical practitioner, his theories false and his influence on modern attitudes disastrous. It is tricky, with Freud, to single out which of his claims has best stood the test of time. Fortunately this is not our concern, here at any rate. Rather, Freud's questioning of the self as something to be known, controlled or mastered will be examined for the ways in which it might deepen our understanding of the construction and deconstruction of the self.

The self, or selves, upon which the interpenetration of desire and culture leaves its trace will form the topic of this chapter. Throughout the chapter, I shall concentrate upon Freud's psychoanalytic conceptualization of the self, paying special attention to the development of various psychoanalytical theories that address the issue of self-experience and self-understanding. The different ways in which psychoanalysis has been used by social theorists and social scientists to develop a critical theory of the self will form the other connecting thread of my discussion.

Psychoanalysis and the Self

'One's own self is well hidden from one's own self.' It was Friedrich Nietzsche, not Freud, who wrote this. Yet it is in Freud's psychoanalysis that Nietzsche's thesis, arguing that, unbeknown to ourselves, our lives are governed by desires and passions, is given its most concrete formulation. Freud laid the foundation for an understanding of the self as radically divided, fractured and ambivalent; he detailed a conception of the individual subject as always at odds with itself. Confronting the demon of irrationality, Freud not only explored the hidden depths of desire but also uncovered the deepest sources of human imagination and creativity. 'Come,' writes Freud, 'let yourself be taught something on this one point! What is in your mind does not coincide with what you are conscious of' (Sigmund Freud, 'A Difficulty in the Path of Psychoanalysis', Standard Edition of the Complete Psychological Works, ed. J. Strachey, London: Hogarth, 1953–74, vol. 17, p. 143). It is perhaps difficult to grasp today just how scandalous this remark was in Freud's Vienna. It is a remark that needs to be set against the backdrop of a Victorian era hell-bent on self-control and self-restraint. In questioning the self, Freud delivered a sweeping blow to the wholly independent self-consciousness of the Western autonomous individual. In terms of nineteenth-century bourgeois values, in which the disciplining of the passions was of the utmost importance, Freud's stress on the self-concealment of the psyche was at once disturbing and damaging. It was disturbing in the sense that, by breaking the equation of self-consciousness and mind, Freud effectively decentred the self in psychological and emotional terms. It was damaging in the sense that, following the Copernican displacement of man's universe and the Darwinian dislocation of humanity within the frame of the animal kingdom, Freud showed the ego not to be the master of its own home. The ego, said Freud, is the servant of hidden unconscious desires. By uncovering the import of unconscious irrational forces for the conscious intellect, Freud rewrote our understanding of rationality and selfhood as shot through with emotional ambivalence, uncontrollable forces and unconscious anguish.

Freud is often credited with discovering the unconscious, but this is not wholly accurate. The age of the Enlightenment brought with it many philosophical and scientific reflections on mental states, such as dreaming, fantasizing and the poetic imagination. Long prior to Freud, philosophers, including Aristotle, Fichte and Schopenhauer, had made reference to unconscious desires. So too, poets – such as Goethe and Schiller – located the roots of literary creation in the unconscious mind. Freud's originality, however, lies in his connection of the unconscious with sexual repression; specifically, in delineating the contents, contours and structures of the repressed unconscious. Repression, says Freud, is the key to grasping the unconscious, and to understanding why many aspects of personal and public life are filled with anxiety, conflict and tension. At the core of Freud's theory of repression is the view that culture places undue restrictions on erotic activity and sexual knowledge. According to Freud, the culture of *fin de siècle* Europe inflicted considerable psychic damage upon individuals; this was a culture which cultivated neuroses and obsessive behaviour through its stringent rules and regulations concerning mastery of the passions. Freud thought modern civilization especially repressive in terms of the relation between the sexes; the observing of social norms contributed to the damming up of sexual energy. Particularly at the level of bourgeois familial life, the burdens of repression were too much – one consequence of which was a generation of anxious women and men increasingly distanced from their feelings, passions and emotional lives.

Most of the unconscious is repressed, according to Freud, which in turn raises important questions about the nature of repression itself. The repressed unconscious, as Freud conceived it, is not a realm of the mind in which thoughts and memories are temporarily stored away and effortlessly recalled; he reserves for this the term 'preconsciousness'.

Rather, the unconscious consists of desires, wishes, impulses and ideas that the self has got rid of by forgetting. Such forgetting renders large parts of our mental activity inaccessible to self-knowledge. This link between forgetting and the unconscious is seen by Freud as primarily a self-protective manoeuvre: when desires and wishes conflict with reality (or, more accurately, that part of the mind that registers the 'reality principle'), bad or intolerable feelings are experienced; these bad feelings are in turn shut away within the self through repression. There is for Freud thus a radical split between the conscious and unconscious mind; the self is barred access to unconscious forms of knowing, thinking and feeling through acts of repression. Yet repression is never complete, says Freud. The desire for gratification and pleasure is as strong as the desire for repression and forgetting. For Freud, this ongoing process of mental conflict can be glimpsed in dreams, symptoms, slips of the tongue or pen, and the distortions of memory.

Desire marks the soul, but in muddied or subterranean ways. Freud thus cautioned psychoanalysts about the immense difficulties of deciphering the mysteries of sexual desire. He was continually confronted, in his own clinical and theoretical work, with the difficulties of grasping the rich and varied ways in which the repressed unconscious shapes personal and social life. This difficulty arose partly because repression functions as an emotional force buried beneath the surface of our daily interactions, and partly because the characteristics of unconscious mental activity are very strange when compared with the attributes of consciousness. Freud described the unconscious as wholly pleasure-seeking, governed by an unbound shifting field of forces in which the boundaries between self and others are indeterminate. The unconscious, says Freud, is radically indifferent to reality, to logic or contradiction, and to time. What this means, in short, is that beliefs, desires, wishes and impulses exist in the unconscious without contradiction – one can simultaneously love and hate parents, desire and loathe siblings, accept and reject friends.

Many critics have rejected Freud's theory of the unconscious on the grounds that, while irrationality is clearly evident from the activities of individuals and collectivities, it is almost impossible to prove that a part of the mind is split off from consciousness under the influence of repression. While some may find this argument persuasive, it is perhaps worth noting that Freud did not understand the unconscious solely in terms of an opposition to consciousness. On the contrary, he argued that everything going on in the mind originally occurred in an unconscious form; it is only later in the life of the infant – and even then only painfully and traumatically – that the mind opens out to consciousness of self, others and the wider world.

Let me develop this point in more detail. According to Freud, the sexual life of the individual, and particularly the psychological process of fantasy, commences at birth. The newborn infant lives in a state of blissful contentment, taking pleasure from any part of its own body, or indeed the body of its mother – what Freud termed 'autoeroticism'. The psyche, he argues, is originally closed in on itself, contained in a blissful world of oceanic pleasure, a world of oneness, narcissism and omnipotence. Human beings, notes Freud, are born prematurely. The infant is born into the world wholly dependent upon others for the satisfaction of her or his biological needs. Food is, of course, the primary need of the infant in the earliest months of life; it is with this firmly in mind that Freud argued that the mother's breast is the original object of longing for both boys and girls – an object that, Freud scandalously suggested, serves as the prototype for the drafting of sexual desire. Today this hardly sounds shocking or disturbing (and many readers may doubt the accuracy of the claim at any rate), but it is necessary to remember that Freud developed his ideas against the backdrop of the repressions of the Victorian era. He contends that the maternal body, or more accurately the breast, provides the infant with the first taste of complete satisfaction, contentment and self-sufficiency. Yet this is more than a matter of biology for Freud. Something else, something more emotional or psychological, is happening in these early transactions between the mother and child. Freud's answer is as simple as it is astonishing: *sexual pleasure*. According to Freud, while the child obtains nourishment from its mother's breast, the experience of sucking is itself pleasurable. Such pleasure, says Freud, forms a kind of template for the development of human sexuality. 'The baby's obstinate persistence in sucking', he writes, 'gives evidence at an early stage of a need for satisfaction which, though it originates from and is instigated by the taking of nourishment, nevertheless strives to obtain pleasure independently of nourishment, and for that reason may and should be termed *sexual*' (Sigmund Freud, 'An Outline of Psycho-Analysis', *Standard Edition*, vol. 23, p. 154).

It is from childhood memories of sexual longing and family romance that Freud erects his theory of the unconscious. At every level, desire always harks back to childhood, to the subterranean realm of infantile impulses and frustrated wishes. In adulthood such childhood memories are necessarily reconstructed through the influence of fantasy; our personal histories and private narratives are suffused with unconscious meanings; our subjective concerns, however much we think we are in control of our lives, are shot through with unconscious ideas, drives and fantasies. As our dreams and daily slips of the tongue powerfully disclose, much in our emotional life is experienced in forms that outstrip conscious knowledge. As Freud expresses this overdetermination of consciousness by the unconscious: 'Thoughts emerge suddenly without one's knowing where they come from, nor can one do anything to drive them away. These alien guests even seem to be more powerful than those which are at the ego's command' (Freud, 'A Difficulty in the Path of Psychoanalysis', p. 141).

One way of understanding the 'alien guests' that populate the mind is in terms of misrecognition, a global distortion in the way we come to think about or, more accurately, fantasize our selfhood as well as our relationships with other people. For Freud's most famous French interpreter, Jacques Lacan (1901–81), the individual subject establishes a sense of self through visual identification with its image in a mirror. In his immensely influential essay 'The Mirror-stage as Formative of the Function of the I' (1949), Lacan analyses the impact of mirrors and reflective surfaces upon the infant's emergent sense of self. According to Lacan, a profound sense of jubilation arises when the small infant sees itself in a reflecting surface. He argues that the mirror provides an image of corporeal wholeness, of oneness and unity. This sense of wholeness or unity is what Freud was trying to get at when he explored the concept of narcissism in his theoretical papers, and Lacan allows us to grasp the importance of the visual or optic genesis of narcissism as a condition of the self. The problem is, however, that the unity reflected in the mirror is not at all what it appears. The mirror is, in fact, profoundly imaginary, because the consolingly unified image it presents is diametrically opposed to the lack of physical coordination that the child actually experiences. In a word, the mirror *lies*. The reflecting mirror, because it is outside and other to the subject, leads to a misrecognized sense of selfhood. The ego or self, says Lacan, is a fiction; selfhood is frozen as an image of something that does not exist.

Lacan's theory of the mirror stage has been tremendously influential in a diversity of academic disciplines, primarily since the theory provides an account of how something outside and other – the mirror – defines the imaginary contours of the self. But note that there is no depth or interior to Lacan's conceptualization of the mirror. One cannot get behind the mirror since we are talking of a pure surface, a flattened image that has its roots in otherness. This is potentially a very subversive idea, since the Lacanian emphasis on the otherness of the mirroring process undermines conventional notions of human nature, internal desires and of true or authentic selfhood. The theory of the mirror stage suggests that the ego is constituted not from the inside, but from without – perceptions of the self are structured according to an external image. Lacan's idea of mirroring makes a mockery of dominant cultural ideas about emotional development, self-mastery and autonomy. All images of the self are intrinsically false, for the self is a delusion. According to Lacan, the original experience of misrecognition generated by the mirror stage becomes the basis of all subsequent experiences of interpersonal relationships, of family ties and friendships, of social and communal bonds and, most importantly, of intimacy and love.

The self that is built up from the mirror stage is an ideal, imaginary projection. In this psychological state, personal identity is experienced as complete, unified and omnipotent; the illusions of the infant's psyche are such that neither self, nor various objects of desire, are defined in relation to social differences or cultural meanings. In Freudian terms these narcissistic fantasies of infancy occur throughout the pre-

Oedipal period, a point at which the small infant makes no distinction between itself and the outside world, between self and other. In order for a sense of social identity to emerge, the child clearly has to move beyond the autoerotic fantasies aroused by, and invested in, the maternal body, and towards a more culturally shaped, symbolic set of relations with parents, with other people and with the wider world. That is to say, there must be a movement away from the early dyadic unity of child and mother and towards a triadic stage, in which the father drives a wedge between the infant and its object of desire – that is, the maternal body.

Freud, famously, calls this stage the Oedipus complex. The child entering the Oedipus complex becomes caught up in frustrating and restrictive emotions in respect of its parents. In emphasizing that the child experiences intense love and aggression at this point of life, Freud sought to understand the complex ways in which the symbolic dimensions of culture are internalized or appropriated by children. Spelt out in more detail, Freud argued that the Oedipus complex comprises both positive and negative aspects. In the positive or heterosexist complex, the child wishes for the death of its rival – the parent of the same sex – and entertains sexual desires for the parent of the opposite sex. In the negative complex, the child desires the parent of the same sex, and hates the parent of the opposite sex. The manner in which desire and defence, love and hate, are organized during the Oedipus complex is crucial, in Freud's view, to the structuring of personality and selfhood in relation to society and culture. Yet if these social prescriptions governing human sexuality seem to fly in the face of Freud's views on the fractured and unstable nature of the unconscious (and there are many critics of Freud who argue that psychoanalysis ultimately reinforces social conventions), it is perhaps worth stressing that Freud was far from asserting that individuals automatically adopt socially sanctioned forms of sexuality and gender. He claimed, for instance, that traces of homosexual object-choice, conflict and identification could be found in everyone. He also believed that, underneath layers of denial and repression, our erotic attachments to persons of the same sex play just as important a role in the development of self as do our identifications with persons of the opposite sex.

Certainly the impact of sex and sexuality upon the psyche looms large in Freud's theories. An absorption with the emotional sources and nature not only of ego boundaries but of gender awareness and sexual difference prevails throughout Freud's writings. Exposure to the intense family drama of the Oedipus complex, Freud speculated, inaugurates a complex, ambivalent relationship with gender and sexual difference: Freud sought to show that the restriction and frustration of Oedipal prohibitions are tied in a fundamental way to the discord of human sexuality.

The main ideas set out by Freud concerning Oedipal experiences of sexuality can be readily summarized as follows. First, reflecting the various male-dominated ideologies and institutions of his time, Freud argued that children of both sexes begin life with an 'active' masculine-orientated sexuality. In Freud's celebrated phrase, 'the little girl is a little man'. Second, he maintained that biological sex difference remains psychologically unimportant until the onset of the phallic phase in the Oedipal drama, at which point sexual difference becomes symbolically linked to the presence or absence of the penis. Third, he argued that psycho-sexual development thereafter follows different emotional and cultural paths for the sexes, with intense anxieties over the acquisition of 'masculinity' and 'femininity' a lifelong problem for the self. Freud rejected the view that human sexuality unfolds according to predetermined patriarchal symbols and structures. But he did advance a general theory concerning the resolution of the Oedipus complex and the dominance of paternal authority: in the case of boys, he said, Oedipal desire is repressed in the face of the father's threat of castration; in the case of girls, he speculated, castration is imagined as already inflicted.

The manner in which the small infant reacts to the threat of castration – a threat which is experienced, Freud reminds us, principally in terms of imagination or fantasy – affects the drafting of the self very profoundly. As regards the acquisition of a masculine sense of self, the boy learns that, while he cannot hope to compete with his father for possession of the maternal body, the possession of the phallus can in time be used to express desire. The threat of castration for the girl's feminine sense of self is more traumatic, however. This is so, according to Freud, because fantasy of castration involves the renunciation of the girl's earlier masculine sexuality. Freud argues that, in the resolution of the girl's Oedipal complex, desire rounds back upon itself – the result of which is a 'narcissistic wound' that leads women to 'fall victim to envy for the penis'. This leads us directly to some of Freud's most controversial claims regarding feminine sexuality, gender and the self. Penis-envy, masochism, jealousy, a weak superego: these are the 'marks of womanhood' as described by Freud, all of which he differentiates sharply from the masculine sense of self. (For a clear feminist discussion of the immense complexity of Freud's account of the psycho-sexual development of the self see Nancy Chodorow, *Femininities, Masculinities, Sexualities*, London: Free Association Books, 1994.)

Freud tried to show, in his writings on the Oedipal drama, that the self is always overshadowed by traces of the family and childhood. The legacy of the Oedipus complex is that, on the one hand, we spend much of our lives trying to discover ourselves and define our experience better, while, on the other, we do this within the tangled frame of a family history shot through with illusion, repetition and repression. It is as if the desire and fear and hate that we feel towards parents and siblings in childhood is displaced and put onto others throughout life; indeed, Freud regarded the ongoing sorting out of projected fantasies from social relations a key task for the self-reflective individual. Yet he was sceptical of utopian claims that the self might somehow transcend the demands of culture and the burdens of social responsibility. Freud's image of the self is one of deep division and ambivalence; it is an image of a world of overpowering emotions and moral prohibitions, of rebellion and subjection, of struggle and denial. Yet there is the failure in Freud to attend equally to the power relations and cultural frames through which narratives of the self are told; we find in some of his late writings an undue privilege granted to conventional morality, the power of established institutions and the continuation of patriarchal sociability. This is the Freud very much impressed with conventional society; it is Freud, the bourgeois thinker, in whom we find, to paraphrase Philip Rieff, the 'mind of a moralist'. This is exceptionally clear in Freud's account of sociability, in which the rivalry, envy and competition of the Oedipus complex is transferred wholesale to a relentlessly pessimistic understanding of struggle and conflict in public life. Some critics, most notably those interested in psychoanalysis on the political left, have sought to challenge these more conservative interpretations of social life developed by Freud and his followers. We will turn to consider some of these critiques later in the chapter.

The Oedipus complex for Freud is fundamental to psychoanalytic theory and its interpretative strength. Oedipus is a structuring emotional event in the life of each individual, an event that generates experience of intense frustration, conflict and restriction. Not one to shrink from grand claims, Freud argued that Oedipal desire is universal; the incest fantasy, he thought, is something that everyone experiences in early childhood. It is perhaps for this reason that Lacan makes the Oedipus complex, or what he calls the Symbolic Order, the crucial link between the mutability of the psyche and the fixation of our cultural repertoire. Lacan, drawing on the latest theories in post-war continental philosophy, transformed the self's conception of itself from Freud's Victorian, imperialistic individualism to a more fashionably structural sensibility. In Lacan's formalism of psychoanalysis, the emphasis is less on passion than of *positioning* in the symbolic order of language. As with others influenced by French structuralism, language is very important in Lacan's refashioning of Freud's Oedipal drama in terms of the symbolic construction or determination of the self. Individuals are not so much creators of their inner desires and worlds than supports of language and symbolic identity. It is process, not people, which counts in the Lacanian conceptualization of the self. According to Lacan, there is a key difference between pre-verbal experience (the world of the mirror, distortion, illusion, misrecognition) and the structure of language initiated with the passing of the Oedipus complex. This difference relates to *psychic structure*: through Oedipal disillusionment, the child is forced to confront limitation, discord, otherness, frustration and restriction. In the acquisition of language, the wishes, desires and fantasies of the pre-Oedipal infant are radically altered to fit with symbolic social structures. For Lacan, as for Freud, the Oedipus complex breaks the narcissistic fullness of pre-Oedipal desire, and locates the child in a symbolic world of language, culture, social norms, legal obligations and duties.

Freud and Lacan are often referred to interchangeably in much contemporary cultural theory, but it is worth briefly noting that there are important differences in their approach to the self. Freud's work suggests an 'isolationist' view of self, in which the small infant starts life closed in upon itself and only subsequently breaks out of the closed world of fantasy to enter social relations. The interconnection of Oedipal longing, repressed desire and moral prohibition is central to the self's participation in the social and political sphere; the lures of fantasy and wishful thinking, in this perspective, are balanced by guilt, the anxiety provoked when the individual does not live up to normative ideals. Lacan disputes Freud's isolationist model, and instead positions the self in communication with others from the outset. Lacan's identity-framing communication process commences with the mirror stage (the confusions and evasions of imagination) and reaches a rehearsal for adult social relations in the Symbolic Order, in which the construction of the self through language results in the imposition of sexual identity. Lacan's theoretical move towards interpersonal relations is at one with a broader trend in post-Freudian psychoanalysis.

I shall discuss further the writings of Freud and Lacan on the Oedipus complex, as well as some hostile reactions towards psychoanalysis generated in feminist circles, when looking at debates over gender and the self in chapter 4. At this stage, I simply underscore the point that the passing of the Oedipus complex is viewed by Freudians as essential to the constitution of selfhood. The psychoanalytic account stresses the *split nature of subjectivity*: the individual is divided between the narcissistic lures of the ego on the one hand, and the desires and dreads of the unconscious on the other. Note, however, that this Oedipally negotiated sense of self is not merely an abstract, disembodied occupier of social roles – as we might find, say, in certain sociological theories of socialization. Certainly the self, as theorized by Freudians, is – with the passing of the Oedipus complex – a fully anchored social and moral agent. Yet the very strangeness or otherness that marks the unconscious is such that there is always a gulf between internal representations of the self and external reality. In Freudian theory, external reality is represented internally through imagination and fantasy, which in turn involves both creations and distortions of the psyche.

For the most part Freud tends to stress competition and conflict in relations between self and society. The shaping power of the Oedipal triangle is such for Freud that conflict and rivalry, desire and defeat, are central experiences of the self. In Freud's version of the self, the Oedipus complex defines the parameters of social relations and the politics of sociability, with identity and intimacy cast as scarce resources over which people battle. This is a highly masculinist model of the self, a model in which self-development always refers back to Oedipal, family struggle, the struggle between fathers and sons for the prized object of desire – the maternal body. Thankfully, post-Freudian psychoanalysis has largely broken with the idea that self-definition depends upon an individual-ist ethos, with its restrictive view of culture and communication. Newer psychoanalytic concepts reconfigure the complex emotional transactions that take place *between* selves, such that self is always implicated with the desire of others. The principal theoretical shift in this connection is one away from the impact of the father, and instead towards the influence of the mother in the constitution of self. The emotional presence of the mother as a resource for the infant's working out of core distinctions between 'self' and 'not-self' has been much debated by students of Freud, and contemporary research suggests children enter into emotional dialogue with the mother from the outset of life.

Perhaps the most suggestive psychoanalytic account of this emotional dialogue between mother and child is D. W. Win-nicott's theory of transitional relations, specifically his idea of 'potential space'. Winnicott argues that mothers learn to combine togetherness and solitude in caring for, and playing with, their children; he says that such a blend of communication, personal space and trust assists the infant in the hard emotional work of learning to be independent of the mother. 'Good-enough mothering' is the term that Winnicott coined to capture this developmental moment in childhood, a term that some feminist authors have been quick to label conservative, condescending or patriarchal. Whatever one makes of these charges, it is interesting to note that Winnicott was, in fact, critical of conventional images of mothering that circulate in mainstream culture. He thought that contemporary images of mothering as idyllic and devoid of conflict were unrealistic and potentially damaging. For this reason he defined 'good-enough mothering' as what happens when mothering in the conventional sense is suspended.

Mothering which is good enough is, for Winnicott, less a matter of the adequate provision of nourishment than being alive to the hopes and dreads of emotional life, and remaining in the presence of the child in a supportive and non-intrusive fashion. Spelt out in more detail, Winnicott argues that presence and silence are central to the emergence of the self. The mother, says Winnicott, communicates by acting as an emotional mirror to the child. Again, we find that 'mirroring' is crucial to the development of the self. Yet Winnicott's description of maternal mirroring is very different from Lacan's theory, primarily because he understands mirroring in terms of transitional relations of imagination, creativity and artfulness. Through her devotion and care, the mother mirrors back to the child his or her needs and desires; as a result, the child experiences a sense of care and containment of inner hopes and dreads. In tolerating and containing the infant's feeling states – from excitement and joy to anger and destructiveness – the mother communicates an acceptance of feelings. The infant in turn becomes attuned to a diversity of emotions, and can begin to express and symbolize inner feelings. The better the mirroring, says Winnicott, the better the possibilities for spontaneity, aliveness and autonomy in the developing sense of self. Conversely, the poorer the mirroring, the less psychic room for autonomy and experimentation, and the greater the possibility for a false sense of self to eclipse normal, healthy development. In sum, mutual relatedness and shared empathy are at the root of genuine self-development.

Imagination, or what Winnicott calls 'potential space', is essential to the creative development of the self. The space between mother and child becomes filled with potential, according to Winnicott, when the former gives the latter chances to experiment and opportunities to create. The teddy bear, for instance, is given to the child as an object for play and attachment. Providing the mother is not too pushy or fussy, the bear can in time become invested by the child's own imagination as something new and original. This is precisely the *potential of psychological space* – taking something that seems determined by family, culture or economics and turning it into something else, something more inventive, magical or personally meaningful.

The psychoanalytic account of selfhood I have been discussing is by no means unproblematical, and there have been many criticisms of Freudian theory. I shall now briefly examine three major criticisms specifically relating to the self.

First, there have been many scathing attacks over the years on the scientific status of psychoanalysis, and indeed in recent times Freud-bashing has reached new heights in both the international academic community and in the media. It is not my intention to rehearse these arguments in detail here (see A. Elliott (ed.), *Freud 2000*, Cambridge: Polity, 1998); but I do want to say something, however brief, about the relationship between psychoanalysis and knowledge of the self. Throughout his career Freud maintained a dogged commitment to the scientific tradition and to the values of the Enlightenment. He sought to develop psychoanalysis as a scientific method for the interpretation and understanding of unconscious mental events in the lives of individuals and groups, particularly as this pertains to the field of psychopathology. Notwithstanding this, psychoanalysis cannot be regarded as 'understanding' in the ordinary sense. This is where many critiques of psychoanalysis as a theory of knowledge seem short-sighted, because of the failure to recognize that the kind of self-knowledge with which Freud was concerned operates in a rather different fashion from traditional, and particularly naturalistic, conceptions of scientific knowledge. At the centre of Freud's approach to psychoanalysis there lies a sceptical and cynical attitude to established principles of knowledge. The conventional idea that science and seriousness go hand in hand was questioned and discredited by Freud; areas of life which we tend to regard as trivial or frivolous, according to him, are in fact central to our ways of knowing, of being known, and to the transmission of knowledge itself. Freud thus devoted his attention to many aspects of life that were often regarded by academics and scientists as unimportant. He wrote about jokes, dreams and day-dreams, the accident-prone, conversational slips ('the Freudian slip'), as well as the uncertainty and unpredictability that necessarily accompanies the search for personal insight. In doing so, he dethroned traditional conceptions of what constituted proper knowledge. He conceived of understanding as an alternative register or space of meaning to that of rationality or cognitive knowledge. It is not knowledge (as ordinarily defined) so much as *transformation* that Freud's doctrines pursue: the transformation of the self, of emotion and affect, of sexuality and desire, of intimacy and personal relationships, and ultimately of social and political relations.

Second, psychoanalysis has been sharply criticized for suppressing the external social conditions that generate personal distress and individual oppression. In this argument Freud makes the fatal error of upgrading the 'make-believe' realm of fantasy at the price of turning a blind eye to wider social forces of inequality, oppression and domination. 'By shifting the emphasis from an actual world of sadness, misery, and cruelty to an internal world on which actors performed invented dramas for an invisible audience of their creation,' writes Jeffrey Masson in a particularly vitriolic critique, 'Freud began a trend away from the real world that . . . is at the root of the present-day sterility of psychoanalysis' (*The Assault on Truth*, New York: Farrar, Straus and Giroux, 1984, p. 144). Masson's criticism is a serious one, primarily because he uses this division of actual and imagined suffering to charge Freud with neglecting issues of sexual abuse in theorizing the nature of repression and pathology. Masson's critique represents, in my view, a wilful misrepresentation of Freud's position – as the latter did not deny the power of trauma, sexual or otherwise, upon the psyche. What Freud did argue, however, is that no experience of the world, however oppressive or catastrophic, is unmediated by the influence of our inner world; social experience is always deeply structured by the psyche – by images, by memory, by hopes and dreads. After Freud, fantasy can no longer be adequately understood as mere illusion, day-dream or escape. Our psychic representations of life do more than record the world: they shape the contours of our experience of the world. Fantasy, argues Freud, is never 'private': it invades and circulates the realms of society and culture. Fantasy is a central psychological medium through which the self engages with the social world.

Related to this is the charge that psychoanalysis is inherently conservative, primarily because of the normalizing and pathologizing orientation it adopts in relation to individuals. The charge here is that psychoanalysis supports an oppressive social order by coercing people in therapy to act in ways more appropriate with public and cultural norms, however stifling these may be. In the view of the French philosopher and historian Michel Foucault, psychoanalysis is a repressive procedure for the confession of sex and for the maintenance of social control. Psychoanalysis is represented as central to the growth of public confession, as developed in self-help books or therapeutic talk shows; such confessional discourse mediates contemporary understandings and constructions of self. Such a connection between psychoanalysis and the confessional – I shall argue in chapter 3 when examining Foucault's theory of the self – is too forced to be convincing. In contrast to the self-disclosure upon which the confessional is premised, psychoanalysis posits emotional blockages and repressed desires in the individual's relation to his or her self. Perhaps more convincing, then, is the claim that, whatever the radical political edge of Freud's work, the clinical development of certain strands of post-Freudian psychoanalysis has been conformist. Russell Jacoby, in a particularly energetic attack, criticizes the psychoanalytic establishment for promising individual liberation and happiness in a capitalist social order that is degrading and degraded (see Jacoby's *Social Amnesia*, Boston: Beacon Press, 1975). There is no doubt some truth in Jacoby's criticism, particularly in a market-orientated social context in which therapy is all too easily equated with caring for the self at the expense of care for others. But, again, there is no reason why social theorists and social scientists cannot draw from psychoanalytic theory in a critical fashion, and thus pursue a politically progressive account of the self and social relations.

Finally, many feminists have strongly criticized Freudians for their replication of patriarchal values and masculinist assumptions. The key criticism here is that the theory of the self sketched by Freud is, in fact, politically and ideologically loaded in terms of gender power. Freud has been denounced by many leading feminists – including Simone de Beauvoir, Betty Friedan and Germaine Greer – as an apologist for patriarchy. Certainly, Freud's interpretation of female sexuality – centred, as it is, on notions of castration anxiety, penis-envy, passivity, jealousy and hysteria – is ideologically weighted in terms of conceptualizing the psychology of self-hood. But more recent feminist theory has cautioned against the complete rejection of psychoanalysis in this connection. In contemporary feminist thought, the interpretative strategy that emerges is one that largely accepts the psychoanalytic account of sexual development, but only on the grounds that this account is understood as probing the profound emotional suffering and oppression to which women are subjected under patriarchal social conditions. That is to say, Freudian theory for many feminists is treated as descriptive, not prescriptive. In this argument, Freudian psychoanalysis represents a powerful examination of the sexual and emotional forces that deform gendered relationships. (The most influential feminist appropriation of Freud along these lines is Juliet Mitchell, *Psychoanalysis and Feminism*, Harmondsworth: Penguin, 1974; for a more recent account see Jane Flax, *Thinking Fragments*, Berkeley/Los Angeles: University of California Press, 1991.) Notwithstanding problems in theorizing gender, many critics suggest that feminism needs to engage with psychoanalytical theories in order to develop a critical theory of sexualities, and to grasp the cultural and psychological dimensions involved in gender transformation and therefore the autonomy of the self. I shall examine the feminist appropriation and reconstruction of psychoanalysis in more detail in chapter 4.

Culture and Repression

Psychoanalysis is very often represented in strictly therapeutic terms, as a clinical practice for curing people suffering from the emotional torments of repression, anxiety and depression.

Freud's brainchild is not, however, a model only for the treatment of mental illness. Psychoanalysis, as has been suggested in the foregoing pages, also offers a powerful interpretative stance towards the wider world – to the unconscious motivations of individuals in their dealings with modern society. Freud stressed throughout his career the intimate connections between psychoanalytic theory and social, cultural and political processes. He regarded the non-clinical development of psychoanalysis as of key importance to the deepening of our understanding of the pressures of culture and society upon human functioning. Analysis of the links between culture and the unconscious is what Freud termed 'applied psychoanalysis', the study of those transformational processes whereby private fantasies become public. And perhaps not surprisingly, it was Freud himself who first applied psychoanalytical concepts to the exploration of literature, art and culture, thus setting in train a line of enquiry that would have important ramifications throughout the social sciences and humanities for the study of the self and social relations.

It is Freud's conception of cultural development that has been taken especially seriously for analysing the nature of social organization, as well as the associated fate of personality development and the self. Freud's interpretation of 'civilization', as initially set out in *Totem and Taboo* (1912–13), posits an intimate link between cultural progress and order on the one hand, and an ever-spiralling instinctual renunciation and repression at the level of the self on the other. Of key importance in this respect is the drive to destruction and violence. According to Freud, the wish to inflict harm on other people, and indeed the desire to destroy, is tied to a primitive, sadistic and cruel dimension of human sexuality. This sadistic aspect of sexuality is most often expressed culturally through the control, mastery and domination of others, which can in turn provide for a sense of self-continuity. There can be little doubt, argues Freud, that our psychic tendency towards violence and destructiveness represents the major threat to the survival of society and culture.

Freud's magisterial *Civilization and its Discontents* (1930) is a book where this battle between desire and culture reaches epic proportions. For it is here that he advances a global model of cultural criticism: the increasing complexity of culture necessarily entails the escalation of psychological repression. The more complex the level of social organization, the more advanced the level of culture, the more the repression of desire and emotion, and hence the greater the need for individual self-control of violence and destructiveness. In Freud's late writings about society and culture, human destructiveness is linked to repression, repetition and the death drive; the drive to destroy is as strong, if not stronger, than the desire for life. In many ways Freud thus expressed the spirit of an anxious age, of a world rocked by economic depression and world war. For Freud, Eros (or, the live drives), lies at the heart of our attempts to fashion cultural order and foster cultural creativity. Eros is the flowering of love, emotional ties, communal bonds and civic association. Alongside Eros, however, is the drive to aggression and destruction: the death drive, negativity, Thanatos.

Of course many have rejected, or have sought to marginalize, the responses of psychoanalysis to culture and society. This has often been done on methodological grounds, the key argument being that Freud reduced complex social phenomena to psychological categories or explanations. This criticism is, in my view, more appropriately aimed at orthodox Freudians, rather than at Freud himself. Orthodox Freudianism, especially as developed by psychoanalysts attempting to pronounce upon social and cultural life, has tended to flatten down culture and history to the level of 'the individual' and 'psychic experience' without questioning the nature of these categories, or indeed the mediation of self and society. Notwithstanding Freud's warnings concerning the conceptual dangers of hypothesizing too quickly about social and cultural matters in the light of psychoanalytical methods, a crude form of 'psychoanalysing' can readily be seen at work in many interpretations of political events – when, for example, issues of political change or cultural transformation are explained away as Oedipal manifestations. Explanations such as these have certainly brought psychoanalysis a bad name. Moreover, it is surely correct to see such theoretical speculation as a defensive use of psychoanalysis, a deployment of Freud to sustain conservative ideologies or oppressive social conditions.

Whatever one makes of Freud's equation of social evolution and psychological renunciation (and I shall consider some of the political implications of this for social criticism shortly), his ideas about culture, repression and destructiveness remain provocative and suggestive for thinking about the self, human relationships and society more generally. Freud's thesis that the projection or evacuation of hate and destructiveness onto others – typically, outsiders or minority groups – as a means of managing psychic conflict offers an interesting purchase on the ubiquity and perpetuation of social violence. From this angle it is perhaps not surprising then that many cultural analysts and public intellectuals have drawn from Freud's global model of repression in order to grapple with the mediation between the individual psyche and society. In a venerable tradition from Herbert Marcuse to Slavoj Žižek, Freudian psychoanalysis has been deployed to analyse the constitution of human subjects in relation to ideologies of racism, nationalism and political violence more generally. In what follows I shall examine some of the major attempts to harness Freud's work to social theory and cultural criticism, paying special attention to issues of personal identity and the self.

One of the earliest uses of Freud for understanding the complex relations between self and society was that developed by Wilhelm Reich (1897–1957). An associate of Freud's, Reich was both a psychoanalyst and a Marxist. In bringing together these theoretical currents, he sought to develop a radical psychoanalytical and political movement in order to address problems of sexual revolution and its realization. In books like *The Mass Psychology of Fascism* (1933) and *Character Analysis* (1933), Reich analyses the neurotic roots of right-wing extremism and fascism; in doing so, he addresses profound issues concerning the psychological impact of politics upon the self. Fascism, he says, does not operate only through brute force. It also operates at the level of the mind – through ideas, drives, desires and fantasies. The origins of the fascist character structure, according to Reich, derived from severe constraints upon sexual desire; frustrated sexuality achieves a form of release by being rechannelled into destructiveness, hatred and violence. In particular, he argues that there are powerful unconscious forces operating between political suppression and sexual repression. Though Reich's work has given rise to various interpretations, the core of his analysis of self-identity can be readily stated. According to Reich, people repress their true selves in order to submit to the regulations and restrictions of modern culture. This is especially the case in social systems built upon systematic inequalities in the distribution of economic resources and political power. Against the authoritarianism of Western culture, Reich argues that the undoing of the repressed energies and sexual drives of the self was fundamental to attaining both psychic health and political justice.

In many ways, Reich was ahead of his time. He advocated the right to birth control and abortion, ran workshops on sexuality and intimate relationships, and was a spokesperson for experimentation in personal life and lifestyle. (To combat the forces of sexual and political repression, he developed 'orgone therapy', a method of treatment aimed at the reactivation of the self's energies and the achievement of 'orgastic potency'.) In other ways, however, Reich's work was naively utopian; much of it bordered on mystical ranting, and his theory lacked analytical precision. For all of his radical assertions about the sexual potentialities of the self, he failed ever to consider the cultural and moral criteria for the evaluation of sexual pleasure; nor did he consider the difficulties of how the undoing of sexual inhibitions might be generalized at the level of self and society.

A related utilization of Freud is to be found in the writings of the German critical theorist Herbert Marcuse (1898–1979). Like Reich, Marcuse sees psychological and political repression as deeply interwoven with the self. In contrast to Reich, however, Marcuse believes that Freudian psychoanalysis – when read against the grain of Freud's interpreters and other revisionists – contains an energizing and liberating account of the fate of the individual in the wider frame of society and culture. Critical of Reich's therapeutic programmes for promoting sexual expressiveness, Marcuse seeks to uncover the emancipatory potential in Freud's own writings.

In one of his best-known books, *Eros and Civilization* (1955), Marcuse develops a critical theory around Freud's theorem that the reality principle entails psychological repression and political oppression. In Marcuse's view, Freud's interpretation of the tension between individual desire and social order is both ahistorical and conservative. Freud was incorrect, he argues, in assuming the permanent cultural necessity of psychological repression. What Freud did not fully grasp is that capitalist society creates a crippling, though impermanent, level of repression. This point is crucial to Marcuse's broader political argument, by which he seeks to turn Freud's interpretation of culture on its head. According to Marcuse, different societies produce different levels of psychological repression. The shift from market to monopoly capitalism has produced especially damaging levels of repression, as the self has become fully incorporated into the rigid, commercial character of economic processes. Yet this state of affairs is neither permanent nor unchangeable. A non-repressive society, says Marcuse, is indeed possible. He suggests that Freud's doctrines point to the possibility of a liberated – a more reflective and more passionate – self. In this sense Freud's theory can be read as supporting political resistance; psychoanalysis offers a gauge by which people can attempt to become more passionate and more reflective about their emotional, interpersonal and moral lives.

The Freudian-inspired social theory developed by Reich and Marcuse did much to bring the insights of psychoanalysis to a wider public; such ideas were especially suggestive in the context of the political demands of sexual radicals' and students' movements in the late 1960s and early 1970s. Yet the ideas of Reich and Marcuse are not greatly debated today, and it is interesting to reflect on why this is so. The short answer is that the psychoanalytic theorem which equates modern culture with high levels of sexual repression – from Freud's *Civilization and its Discontents* to Marcuse's *Eros and Civilization* – seems misguided at best and, at worst, simply wrong. In an age of sexual diversity, lifestyle experimentation and marriage break-ups, the issue of sexual repression no longer looms as large as it once did. The present era not only witnesses a radical escalation in personal and sexual experimentation, but also inaugurates a radical fragmentation of the self and piercing of the social fabric.

Against the backdrop of cultural crisis and moral relativism pervading Western societies in the 1970s and 1980s, the

American historian Christopher Lasch sought to weave together pathologies of the self, disturbed narcissism and consumer capitalism in a bold and breathtaking social critique. Lasch, in putting Freud's ideas to interesting use in his books *The Culture of Narcissism* (1980) and *The Minimal Self* (1985), contends that contemporary selfhood has now deteriorated to privatism, to an antisocial preoccupation with self-image, appearance, bodily self-improvement and personal survival. Western culture, he says, actively promotes narcissistic individuals whose prime concern is the immediate satisfaction of infantile desires. Lacking any personal, moral or political autonomy, narcissistic personalities are emotionally unable to form caring and open relationships; fragile and brittle, the narcissistic self instead seeks out consumer substitutes to fill a profound emotional gap.

Lasch's work was applauded, particularly in the 1980s, as giving some specific psychological weight to the dilemma of contemporary social existence. The central claim of his psychoanalytic criticism is that life today has become drained of meaning. Consumer capitalism, according to Lasch, is very much to blame in this respect since it has penetrated to the core of the mind itself, reorganizing tastes, dispositions and values through the manipulation of mass opinion. On the level of personal relationships, consumer capitalism dehumanizes the self; the self retreats from involvement with other people and the public realm. In the process the individual cultivates a sense of psychic detachment necessary for the pursuit of empty, private preoccupations: style, attractiveness, fitness and beauty. Lasch connects his thesis that the self has become more and more empty to the unpredictability and dislocation of global capitalism. In a world of economic uncertainty, the destruction of old communities and traditions and an increased sense of social exclusion and insecurity, personal identity is rendered weak, fragile, precarious and brittle.

The narcissistic self for Lasch is a direct outcrop of our 'culture of survivalism'. The key task is to keep going, to get by. Life is lived one day at a time. This siege mentality is, according to Lasch, tied to the decline of the patriarchal family. Disturbed narcissism arises as a psychic defence against the failure to internalize paternal prohibitions and restrictions. Fathers are increasingly absent in family life today, and the pressures of corporate life impact upon children with pathological consequences. Left to drift in the symbiotic realm of maternal love and devotion, more and more children are consequently unable to tolerate difference, accept otherness or welcome limits. This is an argument that draws directly on Freud's theory of the Oedipus complex. In Freud's theory it is the father who, in breaking the pre-Oedipal bond with the mother, helps the child to identify with culture. Not so in modern social conditions, says Lasch. The decline of the family spells the arrival of the narcissistic self: this is a self driven by primitive fantasies of completeness and omnipotence, a self unable to make meaningful cultural and symbolic connections, and thus a self deeply disturbed in feelings of self-worth and self-esteem.

The theme of narcissism as emblematic of the meaninglessness and superficiality of daily life in capitalist consumer society has been developed in other psychoanalytically informed social theory, perhaps most interestingly in the writings of Richard Sennett and Joel Kovel. A number of themes recur in such accounts of narcissistic culture: the link between cultural alienation and impoverished emotional experience; the dominance of media culture and attendant selves which find identity only in the surfaces of image; consumption patterns, the interchangeability of objects (goods, services, people) and the breakdown of caring and trusting relationships. In Lasch's account in particular, it is monopoly capitalism and the influence of consumerism that form the institutional backdrop for a debilitating assault on patterns of identity formation.

Various critical insights into changes now occurring in self-development are provided by the psychoanalytic scholarship of Lasch and others on the narcissistic personality. With the development of consumer capitalism, self-identity is subject to an increasing process of dislocation and fragmentation, a process governed by disturbed narcissism. It is the autonomy of personal life that is most vulnerable here, in part because narcissistic tendencies are no longer replaced by civic-mindedness and respect for difference at the level of self and social relationships. As it stands, however, such an account of the relations between self and society is too negative and deterministic for many cultural critics and social theorists to be in any way useful. (See Anthony Giddens, *Modernity and Self-Identity*, Cambridge: Polity, 1991, ch. 6.) For these commentators, Lasch's work emphasizes only the destructive aspects of consumer society, with the individual a clear cultural victim. Yet experiences of self and identity are more fluid and rich than the diagnosis of pathological narcissism can hope to capture. The relation between self and society is not based on a simple one-way flow of power and control (as Lasch sometimes implies), and indeed recent studies of consumerism suggest that culture is experienced ambivalently, involving both new opportunities and new burdens for the self. As was stressed in the previous chapter, primarily in relation to Giddens's thesis of reflexivity of the self, an increasing concern with identity, image and bodily attractiveness arises as a core aspect of post-traditional social environments. Such concerns reflect not a closing down of the self, but rather an opening out of identity.

The limitations of Lasch's cultural characterization of pathological narcissism are equally evident if we pause to consider the relation between self, emotion and desire. In contemporary culture, according to Lasch, self-development is likely to be dogged by a sense of emotional emptiness and despair, from which narcissism offers a temporary, superficial escape. Yet Freudian theory, one might have thought, is more subtle than Lasch's cultural tale implies. Freud himself thought that certain forms of self-love are not only a good thing for social relations, but lie at the core of the involvement of individuals with culture and politics. Emotion and passion, experienced in relation to the self and others, provide for vibrant conduct in social and political affairs. It is in this vein that the psychoanalyst Heinz Kohut characterized narcissism as psychologically essential to the integrity of the self, and highly beneficial to genuinely moral and cultural aspirations. While Lasch acknowledges some of these psychoanalytic formulations in his writings, the point is that it is not clear how his cultural critique can accommodate them.

In contrast, some of the best recent psychoanalytic writing about identity and the self rejects any hint of individuals as socially passive or culturally determined, and focuses instead on the psyche as irreducibly active and creative. Cornelius

Castoriadis (1921–97), in an important reclaiming of the radical potential of Freudianism for social theory, presents imagination as a constructive, creative and ever-flowing source of representations for the self and social relations. In *The Imaginary Institution of Society* (1987), Castoriadis argues that fantasy is a site of multiple, fractured and contradictory positionings of the individual in relation to self, to other people and to society and history. He claims that the psyche is continually elaborating representations and fantasies; as the flow of representations are produced, so new positionings of self and other are defined, which in turn leads to newer forms of fantasy, identification and cultural association. There is for Castoriadis a delicious indeterminacy at the heart of the Freudian unconscious, such that the regulative hierarchies of self, sexuality, gender and power are constantly rearranged and sometimes transformed, at least partially as a consequence of this ceaseless psychic flux.

At its simplest, Castoriadis's emphasis on the creative nature of the imagination underscores the permutation of fantasies and identifications that selves produce endlessly in relation to society and history. We insert ourselves, through the psychic flux of imagination, at one and the same moment as both creator and created, self and other, identity and difference; we draw on existing social institutions and cultural conventions to produce new images of self and society, which in turn feed back into the cycle of representations. In all this, Castoriadis's central theme is creativity – of the individual self and the broader society. Underlining creativity, his theoretical position is a far cry from the insipid, commercially constructed notion of the 'ever-new' in popular culture. What distinguishes his position from popular understandings of creativity is his stress on the open-ended and ambivalent nature of psychic representation and cultural production, and it is this stress which necessarily involves reflecting on the more distressing aspects of violence, aggression and destruction in contemporary culture. 'Creation', writes Castoriadis, 'does not necessarily – nor even generally – signify "good" creation or the creation of "positive values". Auschwitz and the Gulag are creations just as much as the Parthenon and the *Principia Mathematica*' (Cornelius Castoriadis, *Philosophy, Politics, Autonomy*, Oxford: Oxford UP, 1991, pp. 3–

4). It is hard – says Castoriadis – to grasp, and harder to understand, that socio-political paths or fields of imagination stretch all the way from progressive politics to fanaticism and fascism. But the search for alternative futures, and the search for autonomy and justice, are among the creations in Western history that people value highly and judge positively; the practice of critique, of putting things into question, forms a common starting point for a radical challenge to received social and political meanings.

Along these lines, the Lacanian critic Slavoj Žižek (b. 1949) points to the political and ideological boundedness of identity and the self. Žižek draws upon Lacan's Freud to illustrate the ambivalent, only ever half-successful ways in which ideologies of nationalism, race, ethnicity and gender work to contain a deeper psychic sense of insufficiency, loss and lack within the self. Politics and society are taken here as domains that cover over or fill in the split and decentred self posited in Lacanian theory. It is this decentring or trauma from within the self that propels individuals to adopt identities, to try out different forms of subjectivity and ways of life. No matter how much individuals seek to regulate their lives in terms of stable psychic identifications, however, identities remain incomplete. Self-labelling and self-definition, thanks to the disruptive impact of the unconscious, must always fail.

Žižek's version of psychoanalysis recognizes – in a way classical Freudianism never could – that the identity of the self is framed upon a fundamental sense of psychic insufficiency, lack, absence, trauma. What makes communication between self and others possible, so Žižek argues, is the fact that we 'project' conflicting passions and ambivalences onto the space of the other – not merely as a means of escaping painful feelings (although that is part of the reason), but as a screen in order to dramatize social relations. This may sound like a far cry from Freud's dramatization of the self, and I think there can be little doubt that Žižek radicalizes Lacan rather than Freud in this respect. Rather than trace out intellectual influences, though, it is perhaps best to stay with Žižek's fundamental political point, which is that what makes the other, or society or community possible is the intrusion of fantasy, especially the manner in which fantasy screens over the void, lack or absence at the heart of psychic life. The self, according to Žižek, is marked by a 'fundamental antagonism': the self is always falling short, falling apart, fading or failing to live up to some imagined version of identity.

This case is put most suggestively by Žižek in his analysis of anti-Semitism. The Jew, according to Žižek, has long served as a symptom of modern society's own fundamental antagonism, representing a projected negative identity through which inclusive social identities come to congeal over time. This means, as Žižek spells out, that through the projection of otherness onto Jews, society 'establishes' a seemingly conflict-free, harmonious world. 'The real "secret" of the Jew', Žižek writes, 'is our own antagonism.' In this interpretation he seeks to open up that breach or fissure in the identity of the self, a traumatic kernel of desire that may be read in terms of hatred of the other. The figure of the Jew is a particular socio-political creation of the self's fundamental antagonism. 'Society', Žižek writes, 'is not prevented from achieving its full identity because of Jews: it is prevented by its own antagonistic nature, by its own imminent blockage, and it "projects" this internal negativity into the figure of the Jew' (Slavoj Žižek, *The Sublime Object of Ideology*, London: Verso, 1989, p. 127).

In his more recent work, in books such as *The Ticklish Subject* (1999), Žižek has attempted to bring his political and philosophical interests more tightly together through detailed readings of the whole history of the discourse of the self. Whilst the Enlightenment has for the most part privileged rationality and conscious knowledge of self and world, Žižek wishes to speak up for the 'other side' of reason – the excessive, unacknowledged kernel of human passion. From a Lacanian standpoint, Žižek contends that the injuries the self endures in becoming split from the body of the mother – the 'Imaginary' as formulated in structuralist psychoanalysis – are also the precondition of personal and social fulfilment, as opposed to the more mundane business of survival and social conformity. Even so, the 'lack' at the core of desire is such that our pleasures may become warped out of all recognition, always haunted by a primordial frustration that finds confirmation in the more destructive and negative aspects of contemporary cultural life. And it is no doubt because of this very negative view of human subjectivity that Žižek has come to advance a bleak view of the state of society in these early years of the twenty-first century. In *The Ticklish Subject*, he argues that postmodern culture generates a world of 'post-politics'. Post-politics does not mean that politics is dead. On the contrary, contemporary politics is ideological through and through. Žižek says that, notwithstanding the collapse of communism and the rhetoric of the advanced capitalist societies to be non-ideological, globalization has unleashed an insidious inner colonization of human lives, one that penetrates to the most intimate core of the self. Postmodern culture, says Žižek, is jaded. Alongside changes in technology and communication, the functioning of self and society has undergone an implosion of signs, symbols and significations. Meaninglessness – the sense that nothing has value – is increasingly prevalent. As a result, Žižek argues, the self develops various fetishes relating to political and public life: 'I know what I'm doing is meaningless, but still I do it nonetheless.'

Žižek excels at sabotage of the self. His marshalling of Lacan's Freud for political critique, though dense and convoluted, is undertaken with the purpose of returning the self to whatever is strange, to a foreignness at the heart of our identities. Does he exaggerate? Probably; but that is what good psychoanalytic criticism is about – unearthing the evasions of what we cannot bear about ourselves. The inevitability of loss, the centrality of sexual conflict and frustration, the fluidity of fantasy, the inconsistency and contradiction of the unconscious: all of these suggested to Freud a radically imaginary and creative psyche, a self shot through with ambiguity and ambivalence. It is precisely this threatening ambiguity, experienced in childhood, sexuality, dreams, desire and daily life, that Freud's theory of the unconscious recovers for a critical mapping of the self.

3
Technologies of the Self

We live today in a world in which people struggle with changes in sexual mores, battle against the unsettling of relationships, experiment with different definitions of self and search for meaning in negotiating the interpersonal demands of everyday life. Such engagements with the broader canvas of culture in terms of its meaning for the inner life entails the recognition of choice. Choice, in this context, means understanding the active, creative ways in which a sense of self is shaped and reshaped, while at the same time acknowledging the profound influence of other people and of culture upon our thinking about the private sphere.

This concern with the self and identity is, as we saw in chapter 2, often explored on the level of therapy, particularly psychotherapy or psychoanalysis. In the therapeutic context, individuals struggle with complex desires and fears within a shifting emotional landscape; by constructing narratives of the self with which they feel relatively comfortable, the work of therapy ideally leads individuals to a greater emotional openness in the choosing of identities. That is the aim at any rate – although the success of psychotherapy is much debated. Many critics of psychoanalysis, especially those who lament the conformist and oppressive tendencies of therapy, argue against its individualistic bent, its tendency to lead people into the belief that their collective troubles are caused by personal pathologies. From this angle, therapy can be said to promote narcissism, the empty pursuit of individual happiness as an end in itself. When therapy works in these ways, it is relatively easy to see it as self-indulgence. The 'triumph of the therapeutic' (to borrow a classic phrase from Philip Rieff) has in turn produced a therapeutic culture, a world of excessive talk about the self.

Of course, the contradiction between our inner world of drives and passions and our external world of obligations and commitments has been a recurrent theme in a range of analyses in social theory and the social sciences. A classic instance of this pessimistic conflict between social order and personal happiness is to be found in Freud's metapsychology. The securities of culture, says Freud, come at a price, with sufferings, submissions, repressions and discontents. Freud's image of society is one where people need to be forced into accepting cultural order. What Freud was getting at, in so many words, is that personal pleasure must be pressed into the service of reality and social belonging, in order to maintain social order, security and structure. It was for this reason that he painted a picture of the modern social order as always caught up in distortions, illusions and compulsions, since the unconscious continually disrupts reason-dictated rules and regulations. Yet he was hopeful enough to posit a return of the repressed – the entering of unconscious truths into conscious lives of the discontents of modern culture. To this extent Freud is exemplary of the political attitude of libertarian pessimism: he devoted himself to founding a science which held out the hope of a better life for human beings, one free from the constraints of excessive repression, renunciation and regulation, while at the same time, and in a sceptical manner, he acknowledged that authority and passion, law and desire, are inextricably interwoven. Within the framework of Freud's society, more order means more repression, just as greater social regulation means a greater renunciation of pleasure and freedom. In Marcuse's Freudian-orientated critical theory, as discussed in the previous chapter, this heightened assault of power against sexuality and the self is expressed in the notion of 'surplus-repression'.

Yet what if we seek to turn this Freudian argument against itself, and deconstruct the oppositions of pleasure and reality, freedom and discontent, desire and renunciation? What happens if we question the received wisdom that modern social life is intrinsically repressive? Does contemporary society really constrain individual spontaneity, self-expression and sexual pleasure in the manner that neo-Freudians have suggested? For if one looks more sceptically at certain trends in advanced Western societies, it seems that – contrary to the theme of the repression of sexuality – there are powerful cultural conventions which shape self-identity and the self in relation to public expectations about sex and sexual practices. If the self is situated in relation to forms of power and domination, sexuality presents itself as a mysterious force through which the injunction to speak about ourselves, to know our desires, to classify our emotions and to regulate our passions is given shape and meaning in the wider culture.

Consider therapy, for example, once more. Therapy can be seen more in terms of a process than of an outcome or a cure; its method and vocabulary provide boundaries from which the patient is able to produce different definitions of the self, usually by scrutinizing sexual memories, fantasies and behaviour. In reflecting upon our sexual behaviour, psychotherapy offers the means to understand ourselves better – or so it is often argued. Yet it might also be said that the therapeutic task of scrutinizing sexual behaviour is highly coercive, the organization of a network of rigorous social controls by which the individual comes to examine, classify and evaluate sexuality as a major source of human motivation. Sexuality is not liberated when the individual consults an expert to discover his or her 'true self'; rather, the individual submits to a regime of sexuality, a regime defined and reproduced by experts, ideas, discourses and institutional practices. Seen from this angle, psychotherapy is part and parcel of a socially structured set of cultural conventions by which sex and sexuality are subjected to public scrutiny. The therapist in this viewpoint becomes the rapist, imposing psychological controls by probing the secrets of the self. By scrutinizing sexual fantasy and behaviour, the patient is led to believe that he or she will uncover the truth about the self; it may well be, however, that the language of psychotherapy is simply another means for social control, an assertion of power and policing over the behaviour of individual subjects.

Michel Foucault, the French philosopher and historian who died of AIDS in 1984 and whose views I have been paraphrasing here, described as 'technologies of the self' the myriad ways in which individuals engage with the interdictions and restrictions associated with sexuality in defining themselves and relating to others. According to Foucault, one of the most characteristic, and most discussed, transformations that have taken place in Western societies over the past century is the way that sex has been put into language or discourse, particularly the discourse of therapeutical experts, sexologists and assorted psychiatric and medical specialists. Foucault's line of enquiry into the way in which individuals, by their own means, act on their own self-awareness and self-practices in the realm of sexuality has exercised an enormous influence upon social theorists and cultural analysts seeking to develop a theory of the self. In this chapter I shall explore Foucault's work on technologies of the self and consider some of the ways in which his theoretical approach has been developed within the social sciences over recent years.

Technologies of the Self: Foucault

Foucault (1926–84) first rose to international prominence in the late 1960s and early 1970s for his pathbreaking studies of the workings of power and domination upon individuals, and the knowledge that people develop about themselves as a result. In this phase of his career Foucault wrote books on a dazzling array of topics. He studied, for example, public definitions of madness and the rise of psychiatry in *Madness and Civilization* (1961) and *Birth of the Clinic* (1963). In *The Order of Things* (1966) and *The Archaeology of Knowledge* (1972), he offered a history of the social sciences which posited connections between scientific disciplines and the social organization of power. And in *Discipline and Punish* (1975) he examined the formation of the modern penitentiary and the social ramifications of the disciplining of human behaviour. In all these books, Foucault was concerned, above all, with the subtle and complex ways in which social institutions shape the minds of human subjects. By looking at the connections between managerial power, social customs and specific cultural discourses, he developed a brilliantly insightful account of the organization of domination and power as manifested in psychological, medical and penitential practices.

While Foucault's writings on power are not our prime concern here, there are several aspects about his early work which should be noted, primarily since these aspects are carried through in a modified form in his subsequent analyses of the self. Bluntly put, Foucault rejects the evolutionary and progressive ideology stemming from the Enlightenment, which sees modern knowledge as an intellectual liberation that provides the basis for the humane development of culture and society. Refusing to take scientific rationality at face value, Foucault instead sees knowledge as a power struggle, a struggle played out in various managerial languages and bureaucratic discourses resulting in social control and domination of individuals and collectivities. In *Discipline and Punish*, for example, Foucault argues that we can see in the emergence of prisons, social reforms and legislation governing deviance a transition to new forms of discipline and surveillance which increasingly infiltrate different spheres of daily life. In modern society, says Foucault, individuals are increasingly subject to what he terms 'disciplinary power', a power that is hidden, monotonous and invisible. The establishment of the modern prison illustrates this well. In contrast to pre-modern types of punishment, in which discipline was usually open, violent and spectacular, the incarceration of prisoners as a punitive sanction in modern societies is one based on monitoring, observing, recording, training. Prison inmates are, in effect, punished through a process of constant surveillance; the growth of measurement (including classifications, taxonomies and timetables) permits the detailed surveillance and disciplining of human subjects. Foucault adopts from the political philosopher Jeremy Bentham the term 'Panopticon' (which refers to a state of permanent visibility) to define the manner in which prison inmates are subjected to continuous surveillance, and thus a structure of power and domination. For Foucault, the 'birth of the prison' provides the means for the institutionalization of power, the discipline of the body, and the regulation of desire and emotion.

Foucault sees this rationalization of culture as increasingly evident in a range of modern organizations, such as mental asylums, schools, hospitals, and the military and secret services. In contemporary culture, says Foucault, power is imposed upon people through the bureaucratic surveillance of populations, the routine gathering of information and the continual monitoring of daily life; in effect, the modern age is one of 'panopticism', a society in which individuals are increasingly caught up in systems of power in and through which visibility is a key means of social control. Society for Foucault can be understood as a struggle of discourses in which power relations are shaped, with specific forms of discipline and resistance defining the nature of what it feels like to be alive. Those in positions of power, in order to further their material and symbolic interests, seek to gain control over the policing of discourse – of defining what is acceptable and unacceptable within specific forms of life within society at large. But power, warns Foucault, is never fixed. Power is instead best conceived as a relationship, a mysterious force between individuals, groups and institutions. It is for this reason that Foucault often speaks of a micro-politics of power, by which he means the multifarious submissions and resistances of individuals in their engagement with social and institutional life.

There have been several major criticisms of Foucault's thesis that power relations are central to the regulating of society, and these can be briefly stated. First, Foucault's thesis that disciplinary power exemplifies the general nature of power in modern societies is wanting. Certainly institutions such as prisons and asylums are settings in which individuals are incarcerated against their will. However, these institutions have very clear differences from other modern organizations, such as the school or the workplace, in which individuals spend only part of their day. While it is arguable that workplace and school settings are partly concerned with the routine bureaucratic monitoring of individuals, it remains the case that disciplinary power is far more fractured and diffuse in such institutions than Foucault recognizes. Second, in exaggerating the significance of surveillance, Foucault implicitly undermines his claim that individuals can resist or sabotage dominant social forms of power; there is little illumination in Foucault's study of the prison or the asylum regarding the art of resistance. Third, and perhaps most importantly, Foucault's disciplinary society denies the agency and knowledgeability of individuals; the emphasis he places on the social organization of power results in an account of human agents as passive bodies. This last criticism presents particular difficulties, as we will see, for Foucault's subsequent development of a theory of the subject or self.

In time, Foucault came to admit that surveillance is not something that settles upon all persons equally; analysis of the exercise of power, he recognized, needs to be counterbalanced with consideration of how individuals, by their own means, act on their own thoughts, conduct, pleasures and ways of being. He wrote:

> If one wants to analyse the subject in Western civilization, one has to take into account not only techniques of domination, but also techniques of the self. One has to show the interaction between these two types of the self. When I was studying asylums, prisons and so on, I perhaps insisted too much on the techniques of domination. What we call discipline is something really important in this kind of institution. But it is only one aspect of the art of governing people in our societies. Having studied the field of power relations taking domination techniques as a point of departure, I should like, in the years to come, to study power relations, especially in the field of sexuality, starting from the techniques of the self. (Michel Foucault, 'Sexuality and Solitude', in M. Blonsky (ed.), *On Signs: A Semiotics Reader*, Oxford: Blackwell, 1985a, p. 367)

Once more, here we see the importance of recognizing the active place of the self in social analysis; human subjects are creative and knowledgeable agents, not simply the passive victims of social practices of power and domination.

My discussion of Foucault's work so far has been on a rather abstract level, and it is thus necessary to make matters more concrete. A useful way to do this is by looking in detail at Foucault's final, and perhaps most controversial, project, *The History of Sexuality*. Although this project was published in a number of volumes over several years, and while its author seemed somewhat unsure about the overall direction of the project, *The History of Sexuality* provides a powerful illumination of Foucault's key contention that knowledge about sexuality in the late modern age compels individuals to situate themselves in relation to regimes of sexuality, particularly to what is regulated, forbidden, prohibited. 'Each person', writes Foucault, 'has the duty to know who he is, that is, to try to know what is happening inside him, to acknowledge faults, to recognize temptations, to locate desires' (Michel Foucault, 'Technologies of the Self', in L. H. Martin, H. Gutman, and P. H. Hutton (eds), *Technologies of the Self*, London: Tavistock, 1988, p. 40). Equally importantly, *The History of Sexuality* was undertaken by Foucault as a critical appraisal of Freudianism, especially the claim that there is a rupture between the age of repression and the analysis of repression. Considered from this angle alone, an examination of Foucault's theory of sexuality and technologies of the self offers a useful comparison with the neo-Freudian versions of sexual liberation, principally the work of Reich and Marcuse, examined in chapter 2.

In the first volume of *The History of Sexuality*, Foucault set out to debunk what he calls 'the repressive hypothesis'. According to this hypothesis, the healthy expression of sexuality has been censured, smothered and forbidden; at any rate, this is held to be the case in the West. However, Foucault takes issue with this hypothesis, and in fact seeks to undermine the conventional wisdom that sex is repressed. Sex, he says, has not been driven underground in contemporary culture. On the contrary, there has been an ever-widening discussion of sex and sexuality. Sexuality for Foucault is the result of a process of endless monitoring, discussion, classification, ordering, recording and regulation. The medicalization of sexuality, particularly notions of sexual perversion and deviance, has brought into focus the complex interrelationship between desire, sex and power. Questioning the conventional view that power constrains sexual desire, Foucault advances the view that power serves not only to regulate 'sexual taboos' but also to produce sexuality and its pleasures. That is to say, power and sexual pleasure are intricately intertwined.

To demonstrate this, Foucault examines Victorian attitudes towards sexuality in the late nineteenth century. Victorianism, he writes, is usually associated with the emergence of prudishness, the silencing of sexuality, and the rationalization of sex within the domestic sphere, the home, the family. Foucault disagrees. He argues that one sees in the advent of the Victorian era the development of sexuality as a secret, as something forbidden or taboo, which then required administration, regulation and policing. For example, doctors, psychiatrists and others catalogued and classified numerous perversions, from which issues about sex became endlessly tracked and monitored with the growth of social medicine, education, criminology and sexology. These discourses about sex and sexuality form part of a broader realm of techniques for the care of the self in society, techniques which Foucault sees as shaping the mind externally.

To understand the rise of techniques for the care of the self, Foucault argues that it is necessary to connect the West's prohibition against sex to discourses of sexuality in nineteenth-century scientific disciplines and culture. Foucault's approach to the analysis of the intertwining of sex and power is brought out nicely in the opening chapter of *The History of Sexuality*, where he discusses a medical report about a farmworker, apparently simple-minded, who was arrested and then incarcerated in a clinic for sexual transgressions:

> One day in 1867, a farm hand from the village of Lapcourt . . . obtained a few caresses from a little girl, just as he had done before and seen done by the village urchins around him. . . . So he was pointed out by the girl's family to the mayor of the village, reported by the mayor to the gendarmes, led by the gendarmes to the judge, who indicted him and turned him over first to a doctor, then to two other experts who not only wrote their report but also had it published. What is the significant thing about this story? The pettiness of it all; the fact that this everyday occurrence in the life of village sexuality, these inconsequential bucolic pleasures, could become, from a certain time, the object not only of a collective intolerance but of a judicial action, a medical intervention, a careful clinical examination, and an entire theoretical elaboration. The thing to note is that they went so far as to measure the brainpan, study facial bone structure, and

inspect for possible signs of degenerescence the anatomy of this personage who up to that moment had been an integral part of village life; that they made him talk; that they questioned him concerning his thoughts, inclinations, habits, sensations, and opinions. And then, acquitting him of any crime, they decided finally to make him into a pure object of medicine and knowledge – an object to be shut away till the end of his life in the hospital at Maréville, but also one to be made known to the world of learning through a detailed analysis. (Michel Foucault, *The History of Sexuality: An Introduction*, Harmondsworth: Penguin, 1978, pp. 31–2)

For Foucault, the point of this story is that inconsequential pleasures are subjected to the workings of power; he detects in this investigation the emergence of diagnosis, analysis, measurement, classification and specification of bodies and pleasures; through this investigation, state officials and medical specialists attempt to regulate and control pleasures which are, in Foucault's opinion, relatively harmless and innocent.

Foucault sees sex as the focal point of our contemporary cultural fascination with personal identity and the self. By concentrating its gaze more and more on sex, society is able to channel into various discourses a 'regime of truth' in which pathologies and deviations may be read, interpreted, uncovered, disclosed, regulated and restricted. All this is related to science, as the central discourse which influences many variant actions. Scientists – in the form of medical experts, psychologists, sexologists and assorted specialists – deploy knowledge in order to distinguish between norm and pathology; moreover, Foucault argues that in analysing and interpreting human behaviour, science creates sex at the same time as it excavates secrets of the self. The case history, the medical report, the scientific treatise, the questionnaire: these are the means by which science establishes a position from which it discloses, and legislates upon, sex and its regimes of truth. Knowledge and power, once again, tangle and interpenetrate.

At this point it is perhaps worth reviewing the main threads of Foucault's standpoint. His views on sexuality, power and the self have sometimes been caricatured by his critics – so it is important to attempt to outline them accurately. To begin with, it should be stressed that Foucault is not suggesting that the production of sexuality as a process of regulation and normalization is simply the result of external or societal constraint. Rather, his argument is that, while power may prohibit sex in various forms, it also serves to implicate individuals in multiple self-organizations, by inciting desires, dispositions, needs, practices, activities and transgressions. When an adult watches a talk show about marriage infidelities, for instance, he or she participates in mediated talk about sex – talk which is imbued with highly structured rules and conventions, as well as hierarchies of gender power and social prestige. Similarly, people who read self-help manuals about intimate relationships, and how to handle such relationships, are enveloped in a world of instruction as to the protocols of sexual behaviour. Individuals everywhere for Foucault are involved at a personal and emotional level with talk about sex, preoccupied with the cultivation of the self in and through sexuality.

What this amounts to saying, in short, is that individuals today willingly monitor and track down, with a view towards controlling, their sexual feelings, fantasies, inclinations, dispositions and activities. Modern culture in the West has become obsessed with sex as the truth of identity; deviations from accepted adult sexual norms must be guarded against vigilantly. We live our lives against a preconscious backdrop of self-policing. Foucault discerns this shift to the self-policing of sexuality in relation to the role of confession, particularly the need for self-punishment, in the psychological sciences, but also within intimate relationships and the family. In fact, he tells us we have become a 'confessing society'; a society which, through confession, continually monitors, and checks against, the dangers of sex. He outlines a number of more general historical developments in this respect, but the broad thrust of his argument is as follows. The Roman Catholic confessional was a means of regulating the sexuality of its believers; the church was the site in which subjects came to tell the truth about themselves, especially in relation to sexuality, to their priests. When seen from this angle, the confessional can be regarded as the source of the West's preoccupation with sex, particularly in terms of the sanctioned inducement to talk of it. Confession became unhooked from its broad religious framework, however, somewhere in the late eighteenth century and was transformed into a type of investigation or interrogation through the scientific study of sex and the creation of medical discourses about it. Sex became increasingly bound up with networks of knowledge and power, and in time a matter for increasing self-policing, self-regulation and self-interrogation. In other words, instead of sex being regulated by external forces, it is much more a matter of attitudinal discipline, which is in turn connected to issues of, say, knowledge and education. Psychotherapy and psychoanalysis, says Foucault, are key instances of such self-policing in the contemporary era. In therapy, the individual does not so much feel coerced into confessing about sexual practices and erotic fantasies; rather, the information divulged by the patient is treated as the means to freedom, the realization of a liberation from repression.

The publication of Foucault's subsequent volumes on the history of sexuality, *The Use of Pleasure* (1985) and *The Care of the Self* (1986), saw a shift in emphasis away from the modern, Christian world to the classical world, specifically ancient Greek culture. Foucault became interested in the study of Roman morality as a means of undermining the claims to universality of our contemporary system of sexuality in the West. The fundamental difference between classical and Christian sexual moralities, he contends, is that while the latter seeks to regulate sexual behaviour through coercion and compulsion, the former promoted sexuality as something to be self-managed and self-mastered: sexual conduct was something to be indulged in or abstained from at appropriate times. The classical world, says Foucault, initiated a concern with 'care of the self', in which the individual attended to problems of techniques of the self, self-examination and self-stylization. Nowhere was this better demonstrated, according to Foucault, than in the exercise of restrained sexual behaviour both within marriage and in extramarital liaisons. With regard to marital relations, what distinguished the ethical husband was not the demonstration of affection towards his wife but rather the self-control with which he conducted himself in relation to sex and pleasure. 'For the husband,' wrote Foucault, 'having sexual relations only with his wife was the most elegant way of exercising control' (Michel Foucault, *The Use of Pleasure*,

p. 151). For Foucault, the ancient Greek and classical Roman arts of existence demonstrate the intimate connection between self-control and the elegant stylization of sexual conduct: the individual self, in exercising self-restraint and moderation in relation to all sexual conduct, established ethical worthiness and moral authority.

This notion of sexual moderation also pertained to extramarital relations, and Foucault devotes considerable discussion to dissecting the aesthetic values and stylistic criteria governing homosexual conduct in classical Greek society. The Greeks, he argues, did not stigmatize the love felt for a boy by an older man. On the contrary, men were permitted to have love affairs with younger boys; non-marital sex was not considered dangerous or unnatural in the manner in which it is viewed by Western culture, and homosexual bonds did not prevent a man from maintaining heterosexual intimacy and commitment to his wife; the love between boys and adult males was one use of pleasure among others, with different moral rules of conduct and self-stylization. Note that Foucault is not suggesting that the classical age was some golden period in the history of sexuality; for the Greeks, sexuality was at once a source of pleasure and a source of anxiety. Moreover, there were many regulations governing the nature of Greek homosexuality. Older men could engage in homosexual bonds with boys, but not with other, adult men; the relation between adult men and boys was required to be moderate in its display of sexual desire. Indeed, self-restraint and sexual abstinence, suggests Foucault, were central to the ethical regime in which the individual carried out sexual acts. Self-control, self-awareness and self-mastery in the realm of sexuality defined the ethical regime of the classical age; appropriate forms of sexual moderation shaped a way of being, of living, of a whole technology of the self.

In discussing an ethics of the self in the classical age, in which the language of pleasures and the eroticization of the body figures prominently, Foucault came very close to revealing aspects about his own private life and sexuality. In his later years, Foucault was openly homosexual. Profoundly troubled by his own sexuality as a young man, he long considered French sexual culture restrictive and intolerant. It was not until the 1970s, when he travelled to lecture at universities in the United States, that he encountered the affirmative sexual politics of the gay and lesbian communities. The assertion of gay identity and culture fascinated him, and he described the emergence of American gay urban areas – such as Christopher Street in New York and the Castro Street area in San Francisco – as 'laboratories of sexual experimentation'. Yet he was also ambivalent about the gay sexual liberation movement, particularly the assumption that gayness formed a common sexual identity. Time and again, Foucault debunked the idea of a true self; he was scathing of what he called the 'Californian cult of the self', in which the deciphering of sexual desire is treated as revealing the essence of a true self. In contrast to those who spoke of liberating a sexual essence, Foucault argued that gayness meant the *creation* and *invention* of new identities, the extension of pleasure beyond narrow sexual relations to multifarious parts of the body. Such an ethics of the self, Foucault said of gayness, could herald 'a culture which invents ways of relating, types of existence, types of exchanges between individuals that are really new and are neither the same as, nor superimposed on, existing cultural forms' ('Une mise au point de Michel Foucault', *La Quinzaine littéraire*, 47, 1968, p. 21). In linking sexual expression and cultural innovation in this way Foucault is regarded by many commentators as anticipating what is known today as 'queer theory', a radical social theory which deploys the term 'queer' in ironic and strategic ways to question and subvert the rigid hierarchies of masculinist, sexist culture. (The queer critique of identity and the self is examined in chapter 4.)

Foucault's work offers a powerful and challenging perspective on the culture of modern sexuality, and certainly provides a radical political alternative to those who suppose that liberating desire will, of itself, produce a sexually autonomous society. But there are several reasons why Foucault's interpretation of technologies of the self cannot be accepted as it is formulated.

First, it seems mistaken to suppose, as Foucault does, that the historical development of public discussion about sex was uniformly or generally self-deceptive. The phenomenon of the medicalization of sexuality – the process by which physicians, sexologists, psychiatrists and scientists make sex a site of objective knowledge – is significant, and primarily (as Foucault suggests) for its regulation of human bodies, desires, pleasures, actions and social relations. These proliferating Victorian discourses concerning sexuality, however, were not as widely available to people, nor were they as commonly discussed and analysed, as Foucault contends. Medical, scientific and psychiatric journals on sex were primarily consumed by experts in the field; low levels of literacy during the late nineteenth century blocked the wider dissemination and analysis of such texts, and some have argued that even more educated groups were often denied access to this literature. The medicalization of sexuality certainly helped create a new world of knowledge and discourse, but it also functioned to *restrict* sex to expert fields of discussion – which was in turn linked to gender power, of which I shall say more shortly. Another way of putting this point is to say that Foucault too readily assumes that individuals are the passive victims of specific technologies (medical, psychotherapeutical, legal and the like), technologies that establish their deadly weight through a fixed intrusion of power/knowledge into the lives of individual subjects.

All this carries important implications for the analysis of self, and especially the relation between the individual and society. Foucault's concentration upon discourse and language led him, I think, to downplay the creativity of human action as well as ignore complexities of emotional life. In his approach to sexuality it is discourse which produces human experience rather than experience (psychic dispositions, emotional desires, personal biographies) producing discourse. The strength of his position is that he underlines the extent to which individuals, in defining themselves as sexual subjects, become fixed in relation to symbolic discourses and social prohibitions. The making of sexual identities, says Foucault, is always interwoven with a mode of social control. However, the weakness of this standpoint is that it bypasses the psychic make-up of the individual, so that issues of agency, knowledgeability, desire and emotion are not analytically addressed. Thus Foucault's work often implies a one-way movement of power over and above the individual, one consequence of which is that the emotional dimensions of human experience are firmly denied and the self is seen as simply a by-product of discourse. This is certainly true, for example, of his discussion of psychotherapy and psychoanalysis, where he develops a forced account of the links between therapy and confession. His account is forced because, unlike the religious confessional, self-knowledge is seen as inhibited by unconscious blockages in psychoanalysis. This is important for conceptualizing the self because emotional blockages are deeply intertwined with memory, desire and childhood. Frames of experience are at once structured internally, organized in terms of the psychosexual development of the individual and, externally, organized by the symbolic textures of society. In analysing sexuality and the self, Foucault ignores this permeability of internal and external worlds, and downgrades the individual to a mere cipher in the reproduction of the larger social world.

Just as it is often remarked that Foucault's account of power results in a one-dimensional account of human agents as 'docile bodies' and a correspondingly reductive conception of selfhood, so it is sometimes claimed that his subsequent work on technologies of the self facilitates the way for a more sophisticated critique of reflexive self-construction and self-determination. For example, Lois McNay argues that, in the late writings of Foucault, the theme of aesthetic self-construction explicitly emerges. According to McNay, aesthetic self-fashioning for Foucault involves the transformation of the self into a work of art, the recreation of daily life in terms of self-discipline, stylization and aesthetic experimentation. McNay contends that this turn to the aesthetic realm permits Foucault to fill one of the major voids in his work – that is, the theory of the self – in a manner which necessarily must alter any retrospective reading of his writings as a whole. But this having been said, McNay finds much to quarrel with in the manner in which Foucault connects selfhood, interpersonal relations and social change. 'Foucault's conception of the self', she writes, 'remains within the fundamental dynamic of the philosophy of the subject which posits an active self acting on an objectified world and interacting with other subjects who are defined as objects or narcissistic extensions of the primary subject' (McNay, *Foucault: A Critical Introduction*, Cambridge: Polity, 1994, p. 153). I agree; Foucault's obsessively self-mastering individual is intrinsically monadic, closed in on itself and shut off from emotional intimacy and communal bonds. But there is a more fundamental point to be made here, one which I believe counts strongly against those commentators who argue that Foucault's late work offers a radical critique of the self. In coming to the view that the self is an aesthetic work of art which permits a myriad of potential identities, Foucault in turn makes technique, stylization and intensity of practice the key to the governing of selves. One hardly needs to stress the formalism of this view. Foucault nowhere confronts the possibility that self-realization is itself embedded within realms of mutuality, trust, intimacy and affection. His perspective is, in short, an individualist version of the self: what matters is only the intensity of conduct, and in particular the self-control and self-mastering of that conduct. What matters from this standpoint, arguably, is that one must perform stylishly in committing an act of, say, grievous bodily harm, then abstaining for a few months before the next outburst of violence. Little or no consideration is given to how self-conduct impacts upon others.

Second, Foucault says little about gender, or about the intersection of sexuality and gender in the constitution of the self. Sexuality is usually described by Foucault as a realm of androgynous pleasures and sensations; his views concerning sexual self-practices and self-control informed his broader political strategy of desexualization – that is, pressing beyond the repressive confines of gender polarity (male/female, masculinity/femininity, subject/object). However, while Foucault's plea for a redefinition of the body and its pleasures is important, his failure to link the embodied structure of the self to issues of gender polarity and oppression is a significant problem. Certainly, many feminists have argued that Foucault's failure to develop a systematic theory of gender leads in turn to significant political difficulties in relation to a feminist appropriation of his work on the self. 'Any feminist', writes Meghan Morris, 'drawn into sending love letters to Foucault would be in no danger of reciprocation. Foucault's work is not the work of a ladies' man' (M. Morris, 'The Pirate's Fiancée: Feminists and Philosophers, or Maybe Tonight it will Happen', in I. Diamond and L. Quinby (eds), *Foucault and Feminism: Reflections on Resistance*, Boston:

Northeastern University Press, 1988, p. 26). Morris's comment is accurate in one sense, but can be pressed further. For it is not just that gender is occluded in Foucault's perspective; rather, specific aspects of femininity – the constitution of the sexed female as well as the social construction of the feminine – are altogether ignored. This is carried through in Foucault's impersonal account of human relationships: the world of sexuality that he writes about is, for the most part, one in which virile men undertake the exercise of defining themselves as subjects of sexuality. The troubles of sexuality are mastered by men restraining the self, performing desires, maintaining moderation and stylizing pleasures. Foucault's history of sexuality is thus very much in the masculinist tradition of *his*tory: it is a world without women. It is a world in which gender and love have few long-term social influences. The omission is startling.

Let me develop this point a bit further, for as well as reinforcing the masculinist bent of much social theory, Foucault's perspective also carries serious political implications for the analysis of gender power. Foucault's general theoretical orientation was that sexuality should not be governed or restricted by legislation. By contrast, he argued in favour of the multiplication of techniques of the self, the diversification of modes of constitution of subjecthood and sexuality. But what about sexual violence? Surely the state has a role to play in legislating against crimes such as rape? Foucault argued for a time, controversially, that rape should be decriminalized. Informing his comments on rape is the theoretical and political insistence that the link between desire and crime, sexuality and the law, should be broken. If rape trials were heard in civil instead of criminal courts, Foucault speculated, the offence could be considered in terms of personal interests and damages, and thus unhooked from the intervention of the state. Perhaps not surprisingly, Foucault's comments on rape generated much hostility and anger, particularly in feminist circles. Many feminists lamented his lack of understanding of debates concerning gender oppression; the decriminalization of rape, many argued, would be an act of violence against women, an act that would leave women without adequate legal redress and degraded through intimidation within the broader culture.

Finally, there are problems stemming from Foucault's account of technologies of the self in terms of addressing issues of self-reflection, autonomy and freedom. The ethical techniques of the self with which Foucault was concerned in *The History of Sexuality* were those of bodily surfaces, pleasures, sensations. Yet Foucault has relatively little to say about how a new order of bodies and pleasures might produce a transformation in intimate relationships and cultural association. Because Foucault saw individualization as a form of self-imprisonment, and because he viewed the self as shot through with modern technologies of power, he steadfastly refused to consider how individuals might reflect on social practices and, in turn, transform aspects of their lives in the process. The issue of what a better society might look like thus remains unaddressed. Foucault's own answer to this gap in his work was to insist that theory cannot legislate in advance the concrete conditions of social life; to do so, as the history of Marxism shows, is only to court the dangers of political totalitarianism. Rather than prescribing what relationships should be like, Foucault regarded his work as opening a potential space for the individual to experiment with self-definition and self-regulation. Again, however, it is Foucault's failure to discuss the interpersonal, moral and ethical implications of his own studies of sexuality that limits the appeal of his call for a new order of bodies and pleasures.

Governmentality: New Technologies, New Selves

During the final years of his life, Foucault conceptualized technologies of the self and their associated practices of coercion, constraint and domination in terms of the idea of 'governmentality'. In a lecture given at the Collège de France in 1978, he explained that governmentality referred to all endeavours involving 'how to govern oneself, how to be governed, how to govern others, by whom the people will accept being governed, how to become the best possible governor' (Foucault, "Governmentality" in *The Foucault Effect*, ed. G.

Burchell et al., London, Havester Wheatsheaf, 1991, p. 87).
Like the theme of 'care of the self', governmentality focused
largely on the productive transformation of proposals, strategies and technologies for self-conduct. What subsequently
emerged in social theory during the 1980s and 1990s, with
the so-called school of governmentalities, was a style of critique which revolved on the socio-historical shaping, guiding
and directing of conduct of individuals. Indeed, one of
Foucault's key acolytes summarizes governmentality as cap-
turing 'the ways in which one might be urged and educated
to bridle one's own passions, to control one's own instincts,
to govern oneself' (N. Rose, *Powers of Freedom*, Cambridge:
Cambidge University Press, 1999, p. 3). Like many postmodern forms of thought, the Foucaultian-inspired school of governmentalities turned out to offer a dark, oftentimes sinister,
account of social processes – as we will shortly see.

   An early use of Foucault's ideas for thinking about the
relations between self, society and power is that offered by
the British sociologist Bryan S. Turner. In a series of books,
from *The Body and Society* (1984) to *Regulating Bodies*
(1992), Turner (b. 1945) has sought to develop a sophisticated sociological reading of Foucault. But Foucault was a
philosopher and historian, not a sociologist. Yet Turner
argues that there is much in Foucault's work that can be
drawn upon with profit for developing a sociology of the
'embodied self'. The self has been passed off for too long,
says Turner, as peculiarly disembodied; the body is conceptualized in mainstream sociological approaches as a biological constraint upon human agency and social action. However,
Turner sees the embodied self as fundamental to social interaction. The body is something we are, we have and we do in
daily life; the body is crucial to an individual subject's sense
of self, as well as the manner in which the self relates and
interacts with others. The relationship between self, body and
knowledge, says Turner, is central to Foucault's work and,
when sociologically interpreted, provides a valuable model
for understanding the changing relations between self and
society. The body for Turner connects self-identity, physical
self-regulation and sexuality in the context of postmodern
city culture. The increasing emphasis on fitness, hygiene, thin-
ness and youthfulness are central planks in the maintenance

of self-regulation in relation to consumer capitalism. This political struggle around the body, particularly the commodification of body images, occurs not only in relation to the regulation of self and sexuality, but also through legislative and administrative structures. *In vitro* fertilization programmes, abortion, childcare, the medicalization of AIDS as a modern epidemic: it is here that we witness the progressive institutional management, regulation and surveillance of the embodied self in contemporary culture.

In an essay, 'The Government of the Body', Turner extends Foucault's ideas by analysing the regularization of self, the rationalization of diet and the discipline of the body. Diet, says Turner, is linked to a micro-politics of the human body, since it transfers responsibility for the discipline of the self into the hands of human subjects. The growth of dietetics and social science consolidate the administrative management of food consumption as part of the bio-politics of population, in so far as this involves the regulation of individuals, of health, and of mortality. Analysing the rise of expert technical knowledge (medicine, dietetics, social science) as interwoven with the political management of populations, Turner argues:

> Dietary tables were typically aimed at forms of consumption which were regarded as 'irrational' threats to health, especially where overconsumption was associated with obesity and alcoholism. These dietary programmes were originally addressed to those social groups which were exposed to abundance – the aristocracy, merchants and the professional groups of the London taverns and clubs. . . . It was not until the latter part of the nineteenth century that the science of diet became important in the economic management of prisons and the political management of society. The principles for the efficient government of prisons and asylums were quickly applied to the question of an effective, healthy working class supported on a minimum but adequate calorie intake. (Bryan S. Turner, *Regulating Bodies: Essays in Medical Sociology*, London: Routledge, 1992, pp. 192–3)

Dietetics, with its focus on consumption and the body, led people increasingly to care for themselves according to pre-given administrative rules and regulations; it led people to follow expert information in the management and control of the self.

Turner is refreshingly ambivalent about the wider social and political consequences of the complex interrelationship between self, embodiment and gender. He does not see a single source of social power guiding the government of the body/self. Rather, our growing awareness that the body is socially produced and regulated occurs on many different symbolic levels, from medicine to the fashion industry. Like sexuality and the self, the body is today located within consumer culture as a mark of distinction; bodily appearance and control link to the symbolic representation of identity – as a metaphor of society, as a field for gender differentiation, as a site for racial and ethnic cultures and conflicts. However, the embodied self for Turner is not the passive product of institutional and ideological forces, but rather is integral to the very nature of being and of agency in the routine presenting, interpreting and monitoring of daily life. In contemporary culture there is for Turner a kind of lifting of the care of the self to the second power, with regimens of calorie measurement, jogging, and health clubs the means through which people discipline their bodies. From this perspective, the politics of identity is increasingly wrapped around configurations of the body – the fit body, the disciplined body, the body beautiful, body piercing, the body in cyberspace. There is also, of course, the troubled and troubling anorexic body; eating disorders, says Turner, are central self-pathologies of our age. In all of this, however, the body is itself the site of intensified self-management, self-regulation and self-mastery.

The American historian Mark Poster has also used Foucault's theories to illuminate social life in the current era, concentrating especially on the impact of new communication technologies on the self. The expansion of global communication networks today generates what Poster calls a 'Superpanopticon', a technologized system of surveillance. Technological innovation, from computers to the Internet and from fax machines to mobile phones, heralds a new set of constraints and possibilities for self-constitution. The speed of communicational networks today is such that people now 'float' within an excess of electronically mediated communications; like the images and messages dispersed across cyberspace, the self becomes unstable and decentred; in short, media saturation fragments the self. The insidious influence of administrative power and bureaucratic surveillance is crucial in this respect. Poster writes:

> The populace has been disciplined to surveillance and to participating in the process. Social security cards, drivers' licenses, credit cards, library cards and the like – the individual must apply for them, have them ready at all times, use them continuously. Each transaction is recorded, encoded and added to the databases. Individuals themselves in many cases fill out the forms; they are at once the source of information and the recorder of the information. (*The Mode of Information*, Cambridge: Polity, 1990, p. 93)

Poster's account of social relations of domination is one in which the dynamism of technology becomes interwoven with the administration of bodies, the routine gathering of information and the management of self-identity. These novel forms of social control, however, are not imposed upon people from the outside. On the contrary, the emphasis here is on technologies of the self – the methods and techniques by which individuals develop forms of relations with the self, the activities by which an individual makes of himself or herself an object to be represented, regulated and controlled. In this micro-political approach the development of technological media and communication go hand in hand with the technical management, regulation and domination of the self.

The works of Turner and Poster represent intriguing attempts to apply Foucaultian themes to concrete political issues surrounding the self. However, the heyday of Foucaultian studies, conducted under the sign of governmentalities, did not occur until the 1990s. Here the grand master's ideas on the 'arts of self-government' were applied to a whole range of social enquiries – from education and enterprise to crime control and child abuse. Nikolas Rose, a card-carrying Foucaultian, sought to advance investigations of governmentality through a series of influential works, all of which are mostly politically pessimistic in temper. In *Governing the Soul* (1990) and *Inventing Our Selves* (1996), Rose set out to show how the 'psy' professions (from counselling to psychotherapy), as well as medicine, education, welfare and the social sciences and humanities, lead individuals into devoting attention to their own self-conduct, thereby implicating the self within oppressive structures that underpin society. For Rose, governmentality is the power of shaping language – seducing people to conform to what is acceptably sayable in day-to-day life. It is the power of authenticating ways of doing things, certificating modes of conduct, and thus inscribing the self in multiple modes of power. As Rose writes of the relation between the self, truth and power:

> [Expert knowledge] enables us to appreciate the role that psychology, psychiatry, and other 'psy' sciences have played within the systems of power within which human subjects have become caught up. The conceptual systems devised within the 'human' sciences, the languages of analysis and explanations that they have invented, the ways of speaking about human conduct that they constituted, have provided the means whereby human subjectivity and intersubjectivity could enter the calculations of the authorities. (N. Rose, *Governing the Soul*, Free Association Books, 1999, p. 7)

For Rose, the growth of 'psy-knowledges' connects directly with the government of the self and its increasing regulation. During the course of the twentieth century, in particular, the self became more and more subject to 'psychotherapies of normality' – by which he means to say that psychological knowledge became central in how people related to themselves and others, to ways of understanding personal problems as well as in planning for the future.

Rose's work is a suggestive conjuncture of Foucaultian theory, sociology and psychology – interestingly, Rose trained as a psychologist before he moved under the influence of Foucault. His work is not, however, without its problems. Politically speaking, this is a covertly libertarian account of the self, which distrusts virtually all arenas of social activity and uncritically celebrates the 'minority politics' of resistance to the organized and systematized power of governmentality. Rose inherits Foucault's wariness of all forms of social routine, and in the process fails to consider the cognitive anchors that people require to realize and maintain forms of emotional security in all cultures. At the individual level, Rose's Foucaultianism theorizes processes of personal transformation as the result of discursive forms of governmentality involving scrutiny of self and others. From this angle, the individual is not only free to construct new cultures of the self, but indeed is obliged under the force of governmentalities to do so. The difficulty with this standpoint, however, is that it provides no adequate account of human agency, since the self simply appears as the decentred effect of an analytics of governmentality. At the social level, this kind of analysis is generally too eager to overlook long-term historical trends in its excessive concentration on the 'technological' aspects of governmentality. In short, inadequate attention is given to the active, creative struggles of individuals as they engage with their own social and historical conditions. One key reply to this neglect of social and historical structures in the school of governmentalities has been the rather different doctrine of reflexivity, which – as examined in the previous chapter – displays greater attention to the sociological forms of the relation between self and the individual agent than that offered in its French-inspired counterpart.

In this chapter I have presented a critical outline of Foucault's work through an analysis of the themes of self-formation, self-stylization and self-transformation in the broader context of social power and domination. The notion of the self which emerges in Foucault's work connects directly with the process of subjectification, the complex ways in which personal identity is constructed and subsumed by social forces. Foucault's dissection of sexuality and the self was introduced in the context of a more broad-ranging discussion of various therapeutical developments, in particular psychoanalysis, as a means of tracing the normalizing forces that impact upon individuals in the construction of identity. Foucault's general idea that the Christian prohibition against sex, and especially discussion about sexuality, was actually contrary to the normative inducement to talk of sex (either at the confessional or at therapy) was examined and critically analysed. I argued that Foucault's work provides a novel and interesting guide to the ways in which 'sex talk' saturates our culture, and in particular influences the ways in which people think about their sexual feelings and inner worlds. I raised a number of conceptual and political difficulties, however, with the idea that psychoanalytic therapy is used merely to control individuals, especially those individuals who deviate from adult sexual norms. I suggested that, in the case of psychoanalysis at any rate, this model is scarcely adequate for an understanding of the self, sexuality and sexual oppression. While Foucault views psychotherapy as indicative of society's ever more refined techniques of subjection and surveillance, the problem with this approach to the concepts of self and identity is that it remains top-heavy, suggesting a view of the subject overdetermined by the motions of power. It is in order to theorize identity beyond the normalizing process of objectification that Foucault develops the idea of 'technologies of the self'. This manoeuvre permits Foucault to theorize forms of individuality, and in particular the multiplicity of ways in which individuals constitute their identities in a creative and constructive fashion, and at the same time identify those modalities of power that constrain, limit or repress forms of self-expression. This model of subjectivity, combining the positivity and negativity of forms of identity formation, is in turn linked to an analysis of the broader discursive power relations operating within modern societies.

While a turn to the notion of aesthetic transformation enables Foucault to reconceptualize the attainment of autonomy in his late writings, it remains the case that most sociologists and social theorists indebted to Foucault draw from his analysis of power relations that permeate the social realm in order to understand processes of subjectification and normalization of the self. In the case of the sociological writings of Turner and the historical studies of Poster, Foucault is deployed to dislocate the rigid identity logic that grips modern rationality and thereby eradicates the space for the negotiation of difference or otherness at the level of identity. Foucault's critique of Enlightenment rationality and of the rational subject of modernity thus remains of immense critical value to the social sciences in its broad conclusions. But, despite the various ways in which Foucault's critique of the self has been drawn upon in the social sciences, I have suggested that this conception of the self is not without certain theoretical limitations – to do with the conceptualization of creativity and autonomy at the level of subjectivity in particular, but also in terms of conceptualizing the self in relationship with others and interpersonal relationships. Throughout the chapter I have noted that Foucault's analysis of the self regularly privileges forms of self-mastery and self-governance that would appear to be premised on an unexamined and nostalgic vision of masculine subjectivity. In this connection, the Foucaultian critique of the subject may have more in common with the Enlightenment notion of the self than his followers may readily acknowledge. To say this is to draw attention to the missing element of gender in Foucault's discussion of the self. Like many of the sociological approaches to identity that I have looked at, as well as some of the unexamined assumptions influencing the psychoanalytic conceptualization of identity, the Foucaultian account of selfhood appears to rest upon particular forms of male experience, forms of experience that privilege the masculine self over relations with feminine others. Whatever one makes of these particular criticisms, the theme of gender provides a convenient transition to the next chapter.

4
Self, Sexuality and Gender

Contemporary feminist debate constitutes a rich and fruitful terrain of interdisciplinary research on the self and identity. Feminists have in recent years drawn from, and helped to revise, diverse theoretical currents for analysing the self – from psychoanalysis to queer theory. Feminists have been especially preoccupied with investigating the deep and lasting connections between self, sexuality and patriarchy – the dominance of male power within gender relations and in the context of other social institutions. This chapter examines some of these theoretical exchanges. I shall begin by discussing the integration of feminist and psychoanalytical perspectives for the critique of the self. I shall subsequently turn to explore the shifts and divisions in recent feminist debate concerning the constitution of self in relation to sexuality, desire and gender.

Feminism and Psychoanalysis: Two Recent Views

Feminists view the relation between gender and self as a core political issue. Human beings are born male and female, but become men and women through a process of social construction. Gender reproduction, a term used by social scientists to describe the ways in which people are constituted as sexed individuals, is bound up with cultural forces of socialization, role learning and gender stereotyping. However, feminist research highlights that gender awareness involves more than the impersonal rules and regulations of socialization. To brush against gender conflicts and divisions is to experience something deeply unsettling within the self. For in the earliest years of life, gender is powerfully lodged within the psyche; the child's developing sense of self reflects a meshing of emotional, private and interpersonal worlds. These worlds are closely tied to gender relations in the family.

One of the most debated issues in contemporary feminism concerns the child's early experiences of mothering. Feminists have been particularly preoccupied with analysing the complex links between women's mothering and patriarchal social relations. For some feminists, mothering – as refracted through the patriarchal family – is deeply interwoven with the production and reproduction of gender domination. The centrality of women's mothering to shaping the psychology of the self is intimately interwoven with the perpetuation of sexual difference and gender inequality. Anxieties about mothering are very deeply entrenched in our society, and are reflected in the simultaneous idealization and denigration of women in cultural representations of mothering, in advertising, the mass media and popular culture, and in images of romantic love and domestic life.

While some writers have valorized motherhood as indicative of women's superior biological capacities, feminists have for the most part lamented the ways in which mothering has been socially and culturally circumscribed. In her celebrated book *The Second Sex*, the French feminist philosopher Simone de Beauvoir presented a devastating indictment of our society for its cultural denigration of women, childbirth and mothering. In de Beauvoir's eyes:

> [Woman – oppressed and marginalized – does] not know the pride of creation; she felt herself the plaything of obscure forces, and the painful ordeal of childbirth seemed a useless or even troublesome accident. But in any case giving birth and suckling are not activities, they are natural functions; no project is involved; and that is why woman found in them no

> reason for a lofty affirmation of her existence – she submitted
> passively to her biological fate. . . . It is male activity that in
> creating values has made of existence itself a value; this activ-
> ity has prevailed over the confused forces of life; it has subdued
> Nature and Woman. (Simone de Beauvoir, *The Second Sex*,
> Harmondsworth: Penguin, 1984, pp. 94–7)

Male rationality and logic are contrasted with womanhood
and female biology by de Beauvoir. The dichotomy between
male activity and female passivity, she argues, informs
dominant cultural representations of sexuality and gender.
Although the points at issue here are complex, and many
remain divided about them, the feminist analysis of mothering has in turn drawn inspiration from de Beauvoir's account
of gender hierarchy in order to recover women's creative
power and potential in childbearing and parenting. The
argument is not that a wider cultural appreciation of the
importance of mothering will in itself transform embattled
gender relationships. But much current research does focus
on the emotional connection and continuity established in the
mother–child relation, and examines critically the possibilities for social transformation as a result of the overcoming
of society's widespread cultural denigration of women's work
as mothers.

The theoretical dialogue between feminism and psychoanalysis has been especially important to the analysis of
mothering and its cultural consequences. For many feminists,
Freud's critique of social and sexual repression is crucial to
understanding the dynamics of sexual difference and gender
hierarchy. Following Freud, feminists have affirmed that the
child who emerges from the Oedipus complex is securely
locked within gender division, a self located within a system
of male-dominated heterosexual social relations, an individual whose desires are channelled towards sexual reproduction
– thanks to the unconscious force of anxious and paranoid
projections. More troubling to feminism, of course, is Freud's
grounding of gender in relation to the presence or absence of
the phallus. As discussed in chapter 2, the possession of the
phallus in Freud's theory is symbolically tied to the achievement of masculinity, while the absence of the phallus remains
the mark of femininity. In making gender identity dependent

upon genital perception, Freud's theory, some critics say, reduces issues about the social construction of sexuality to biological or anatomical distinctions. However, such an argument seems difficult to sustain. Freud was very careful to guard against biological reductionism, and indeed his account of sexuality stressed the plasticity and diversity of sexual desire, fantasy and orientation. 'Polymorphous perversity', defined by Freud as the core of human sexuality, means there is an enormous fluidity of sexual desires, orientations, dispositions and practices.

What is certainly problematic in Freud's work, however, is the emphasis placed upon the father as agent of separation and individuation for the developing child. It is this emphasis on the father as the foundation of gender difference and division that has been forcefully challenged in recent feminist psychoanalytic work, especially in the United States and Europe. By turning Freud's theory against itself, feminist psychoanalytic critics have sought to concentrate instead on the mother–child relation. Here the argument is that symbolic representations of masculinity and femininity are derived from the infant's attachment to its mother. In psychological terms, the mother, more than the father, influences the child's experience of gender, or this is so at any rate during the first few years of life because of the closer emotional bond established during infancy. This idea of the power of the mother as the central developmental force for the child has been developed most forcefully by the American feminist sociologist Nancy Chodorow (b. 1944), a writer influenced by the object-relations school of psychoanalysis. In Chodorow's feminist theory, female mothering serves as a driving psychological force in the reproduction of male and female personality. The role of the father in determining gender identity accordingly shifts to the background in this account. An examination of Chodorow's theory will provide a useful entry point into psychoanalytically orientated feminist theory, and will also set the scene for the subsequent comparison of her work with a European feminist interpretation of mothering and its consequences for gender identity and the self.

In her landmark book *The Reproduction of Mothering* (1978), Chodorow contends that exclusive female mothering leads to gender oppression. In her view, women's mothering is pivotal for understanding gender development and division since it is a global feature of the sexual division of labour. Chodorow argues that, in mothering, women become primarily preoccupied with emotional and relational issues; women turn their energies to the care of their children and families. By contrast, men work in the cold and detached world of public and economic affairs. As men are less connected to their emotional lives, they develop more analytical modes of relating to others and the wider society. Chodorow says that we need to know more about this division of gender roles, and accompanying sense of self, in order to understand the cultural logic of gender hierarchy and to contest oppressive social relationships.

According to Chodorow, Freud's model of gender development – in which the mother hovers in the background – is unconvincing at best and plainly defective at worst. In situating the mother as the first emotional attachment for the child, Freudian theory opened up a fertile research area relating to the emotional consequences of maternity. Yet mothers, paradoxically, are accorded little recognition in shaping the psychology of the self in Freud's writings. Instead, the child's attachment to the mother is broken up through the intrusive impact of the father – which Freud theorized in terms of the Oedipus complex. The symbolic intervention of the father, represented by the phallus, into the mother–child dyad is fundamental to the constitution of selfhood, gender, sexuality, meaning, rationality and culture. Freud's theory is essentially father-centred; mothers do not get much recognition for their input into self or gender development. Rejecting what she sees as the patriarchal assumptions of classical Freudian theory, Chodorow turns to object-relational theories of psychoanalysis and also to theories of core gender identity. In doing so, she develops a perspective that examines not only the infant's needs and desires in its earliest years (as with classical Freudian theory), but also the desires for, and behaviour towards, the child experienced by parents. The constitution and development of self and gender, says Chodorow, involves a two-way traffic – between parents and child.

It is Chodorow's contention that the creation of self and gender depends upon the internalization – an emotional taking in or incorporation – of imagery of the mother. In the early pre-Oedipal period, where the father does not figure as a strong emotional presence, the process of gender differentiation is set in train by the mother's mode of relating to, and interaction towards, her child. This brings us to the core of Chodorow's argument: *mothers relate to daughters in a fashion that they do not to sons.* The mother, Chodorow says, relates to her daughter as an extension of herself, as a double, as belonging to the same gender. As daughters are treated by mothers as the same, the daughter in turn finds it extremely difficult to separate from her mother, to establish a sense of personal identity and autonomy. The consequences of this are complex. Chodorow suggests that daughters are likely to grow up with a strong sense of emotional continuity with their mothers. This sense of continuity provides for intimate, relational connections throughout women's adult lives, but it also results in problems of merging with others, difficulties with interpersonal boundaries, and disturbances of self and identity. All this serves to drive the daughter from the love of her mother to the security offered by her father; this subsequent and defensive identification with the father serves as an unacknowledged support for oppressive gender relations and patriarchy.

The sense of sameness imposed by mothers upon their daughters stands in marked contrast to the projection of difference and otherness onto sons. Boys, according to Chodorow, separate more easily than do girls because the mother treats the male child as different, as a member of the other gender. Here masculinity is constituted by maternal disengagement: the mother, because of the child's otherness, propels the boy towards differentiation and individuality. Boys must learn to deny their primary emotional attachment to the mother. By turning away from their emotional dependence on the mother, boys direct their energies to more active, and very often aggressive, forms of play and relationship. In doing so boys, with the help of their mothers, begin to prepare for the sort of emotional detachment and analytical form of reasoning that the economic world of capitalism will demand from them in later life.

If Chodorow sometimes worries that gender identity is not as clear-cut as her theory implies – what of lesbian mothers? what influence do house-husbands wield? what impact do siblings have? – the story that emerges from her book about the emotional roots of women's mothering is forceful and compelling. Since the emotional core of feminine identity is relational – that is, there is a strong preoccupation with issues of nurturance, care, empathy and relatedness – women will tend to look for such emotional resources in other people in their adult relationships. But here women run into difficulties. Since men are very often emotionally detached and unresponsive to more reflective and caring relationships, women routinely find themselves cut off from interpersonal communication and erotic intimacy with their partners. In order to escape from this emotional deadlock, women turn instead to the prospects and challenges of motherhood. Chodorow thus suggests that the desire to mother is, in part, produced from current distortions and pathologies of gender hierarchy. Against this bleak assessment, she urges shared parenting as a means of challenging and subverting the reproduction of gender difference and hierarchy.

Chodorow's work represents one of the most sociologically engaged feminist attempts to analyse gender division and the social structure in which the mothering role is reproduced by women. Her account of core gender identity – that is, socially induced psychological constructions of femininity and masculinity – is appealing because of its potentially wide application. Questions concerning the gender discriminations and orientations of science; problems relating to public policy and parenting; and debates in respect of differences in the moral and ethical outlooks of men and women: all are important areas of social research that have been bolstered in recent years by Chodorow's portrait of feminine and masculine personality.

However, Chodorow's work has met with some harsh criticisms, especially from other psychoanalytically orientated feminists. Jacqueline Rose, for example, has suggested that Chodorow does not explain the psychodynamics of sexual identity and selfhood, but rather addresses the question of gender roles. For Rose, Chodorow's work displaces the core psychoanalytic concepts of fantasy and the unconscious in favour of a sociological notion of 'gender imprinting'. The psychic lives of women and men, Rose points out, are more contradictory or split than Chodorow's theory suggests. So too, Janet Sayers and Lynne Segal have argued that Chodorow tends to conflate femininity with motherhood. Female desire is thus analytically erased.

There are, in my view, important difficulties here. Chodorow says little about the structure of sexual difference and the unconscious determinants of individual subjectivity, sexual orientation, desire and fantasy. She tends to assume that the mother's manner of relating to her daughter or son is fairly consistent with established gender norms, and that these patterns of relating will have very clear-cut and uniform emotional consequences at the level of the self. But we need to be careful about assuming that the emotional reactions and responses of children to others can be interpreted with reference to parental or cultural norms. We need to be careful because, as Freud and other psychoanalysts after him argue, the child experiences the mother in and through fantasy, as well as other cognitive modes of understanding. This is such a key aspect of psychoanalytic theory that its neglect by Chodorow represents a serious omission. That mothers perceive, on a deep psychological level, their daughters as the *same* as themselves is surely evidence of the psychological importance of sexual difference and its cultural structure; the ways in which fantasy shapes, distorts or transforms this psychological and cultural structure requires analysis.

Here Freud's theory of the Oedipus complex and Lacan's emphasis on language and symbolism are important. In Freud and Lacan it is the father's phallus, as the mark of sexual difference, that separates the child from the maternal body and plunges her or him into the order of language and the world of symbolism. In this approach desire is founded in language – the sexes are organized around linguistic shifters – 'femininity' and 'masculinity', 'woman' and 'man', 'his' and 'hers'. Chodorow, by contrast, sees the mother as playing a more central role in the establishment of gender identity, and her use of object-relations theory to analyse emotional connection and separation offers a substantial correction to the father-centred perspectives of Freud and Lacan. Yet reversing the Freudian emphasis from the father to the mother is hardly a radical political gesture unless the question of sexual difference is itself raised and problematized. Chodorow, it might be said, fails to see that the psychoanalytical theory she draws from is itself problematically inscribed within patriarchy.

As discussed in chapter 2, Freud's writings demonstrate the degree to which the young infant's mind produces, in fantasy, desires and wishes that, in reality, are forbidden or prevented from being given external expression. Freud's work has triggered a range of varying intellectual debates about the ways in which fantasy, desire, meaning and biography are brought into relationship, as well as given coherence and structure over time. The relationship between fantasy and gender has been especially topical in recent feminist debates about the self. In what follows I shall use as a basis for comparison with Chodorow's theory of the reproduction of mothering the work of a social theorist who has had a significant impact in gender studies and feminism. The writings of the French feminist psychoanalyst Julia Kristeva (b. 1941) are of considerable interest to the present discussion because, in reworking Freud's account of fantasy as it relates to gender and the self, she develops an analysis of women's mothering that is in marked contrast with that of Chodorow.

In a series of provocative essays about mothering and childbirth – most importantly 'Stabat Mater', 'Motherhood According to Bellini', and 'From One Identity to an Other' – Kristeva analyses both dominant cultural representations of maternity and the psychic experience of motherhood itself. In some respects, Kristeva's objectives in these essays are much the same as those of Chodorow: to examine scientific understandings of motherhood and femininity (with specific reference to the issue of the psychic roots and motivations of mothering), and to consider the implications of Freud's writings for research into maternity. But while Chodorow argues that a good deal of Freud's theory concerning the intertwining of fantasy, sexuality and gender is unsatisfactory, Kristeva (while nonetheless critical of the patriarchal assumptions that inform Freud's writings) argues that the psychoanalytical concept of fantasy is of core importance for grasping the complexity of maternity, and especially the complex emotional dynamic between mother and child.

Kristeva suggests that dominant scientific understandings of maternity, from the cult of the Virgin in Christian theology to media images of women in popular culture, have

objectified women. When femininity and maternity are con-
flated, she argues, the mother's desire exists only in so far as
it is related to her desire to have children, to reproduce the
species, to fulfil her biological function in the name of patriarchy. While Kristeva does not specifically discuss Chodorow's work, it is clear enough from her conceptual approach
that Chodorow's emphasis on maternal reproduction and
gender relationships precludes serious analysis of the fantasies and fears that shape the mother's desire. That is to say,
Chodorow's treatment of mothering evacuates maternal
desire in its exclusive concentration on patterns of relating to
daughters and sons. By contrast, Kristeva seeks to investigate
the relationship between feminine desire and maternal fantasy,
and specifically how this relation affects the constitution of
the self.

Kristeva focuses on *fantasies* of maternity rather than *practices* of motherhood. In doing so, she makes explicit her debt
to the Freudian conceptualization of the self. Sha suggests
that, although maternity has been disfigured by patriarchy,
motherhood is in fact associated with repressed desire. Let
me sketch in what this provocative argument involves. Freud
regarded maternity as a return of the repressed, a return of
the daughter's buried wish to bear a child for her own father.
Fundamental to Freud's view is the presumption that women's
desire exists only in so far as it is directed towards the phallus
– that is to say, the symbolic father of the Oedipus complex.
According to Kristeva, Freud constructed maternity in wholly
patriarchal terms. But this association of motherhood with
the masculine logic of Oedipus prevents the woman from
voicing her own desire, her own enjoyment, her own ambivalent fantasy of maternity. For Kristeva, motherhood must be
approached differently, in a fashion other than that emphasized in philosophical, literary and psychoanalytic traditions,
with their stress upon biological and social reproduction.

In 'Stabat Mater', a title that refers to the anguish of the
Virgin Mary at the crucifixion, Kristeva reflects on her own
experience of pregnancy and birth. Dividing the essay into
two discourses, she writes on one side of the page of the
mythical language of Christian theology and the rationality
of science, while, on the other side, she develops a more
private and autobiographical account of motherhood. In

dividing the narrative of her essay in this way, Kristeva seeks to underscore the split or hiatus between the ideal and actuality of maternity. Most importantly, she argues that splitting itself defines maternal experience. Maternity for Kristeva involves a state of radical paradox, of heterogeneity, of singularity and plurality, of sameness and difference. In Kristeva's words:

> A mother is a continuous separation, a division of the very flesh. And consequently a division of language – and it has always been so. Then there is this other abyss that opens up between the body and what has been its inside: there is the abyss between the mother and the child. What connection is there between myself, or even more unassumingly between my body and this internal graft and fold, which, once the umbilical cord has been severed, is an inaccessible other? . . . Trying to think through that abyss: staggering vertigo. No identity holds up. (*The Kristeva Reader*, Oxford: Blackwell, 1986, pp. 178–9)

Kristeva's analysis of the emotional currents underpinning pregnancy and motherhood contrasts with that offered by Chodorow. The latter tends to present the relation between the mother and her child as fully shaped by relational patterns, gender dispositions and ideological preconceptions. But for Kristeva pregnancy and the maternal body call into play deeper unconscious forces, reawakening the repressed division between word and flesh, representation and imagination, culture and nature. As the paragraph quoted from Kristeva above indicates, the passion of maternity splits the woman between identity and its collapse, between consciousness of self and its erasure.

The mother's experience of transformations occurring in her own body during pregnancy reorient her away from the narrow confines of masculine logic and patriarchy. Whereas Freud sees maternity as an expression of repressed paternal longings, in Kristeva's eyes the desire to have children is itself a sublimated desire to recover the maternal body. That is to say, Kristeva suggests that there is a homosexual component implicit in women's desire to mother, or at least this is so in fantasy. 'By giving birth,' writes Kristeva, 'the woman enters into contact with her mother; she becomes, she is her own mother.' In underscoring this homosexual facet of mother-hood, Kristeva rewrites psychoanalysis away from the father and the Oedipus complex and towards the (imaginary) relation between women, a relation that persists over time and across generations.

Kristeva connects the complexity and heterogeneity of maternal experience not only to women, but also to the emotional development of children. She emphasizes the importance of maternity in shaping and regulating the emerging self prior to entry into the Oedipus complex – in which the acquisition of language, rationality and sexual subjectivity occurs. This is a very important aspect of Kristeva's argument, an aspect that directly challenges the claim advanced by Freud and Lacan that it is the father alone who propels the child into an order of language and symbolism. By contrast Kristeva argues that the mother imposes a sense of regulation and order upon the child's psychic world. Before 'the Law of the Father' (Lacan), the child constantly encounters various maternal regulations, what Kristeva terms 'the law before the law'. Whereas Freudians and Lacanians view the regulation of the self in terms of rationality or structure, Kristeva emphasizes the importance of the body to the constitution of the self. The mother, says Kristeva, regulates what goes into, and also what is evacuated from, the child's body. This maternal regulation and control of the infant's traffic with both nourishment and love provides a foundation for the emotional dealings of the self with itself, other people, and the wider society.

At this point it might be useful to sum up the preceding discussion. Kristeva's writings on aspects of maternal fantasy serve as a useful corrective to Chodorow's critique of mothering. According to Kristeva, fear of ambivalence plays a key role in the ways in which women experience motherhood; this fear can, in turn, fuel the transmission of coercive gender identities in interactions of the child with the mother. To understand adequately how repressed or disowned desires of maternity enter into asymmetrical relations of gender power, however, we need to connect Kristeva's narrative to some version of Chodorow's account of historically specific forms of gender relation. That is to say, we need a critical theory of both maternal fantasy and actual maternal behaviour, one with sufficient sociological and historical depth to capture the positioning of motherhood in relation to gender power and sexual division. This may seem a tall order, but feminist debate in recent years suggests that neither Chodorow nor Kristeva fully grasps the connecting threads between fantasy and culture, women's desire and patriarchal bonds of love.

By contrast, a new feminism that arose in the 1990s, on both sides of the Atlantic, offers a very different purchase on the self, one in which the conceptual mixing of desire and discourse is given due prominence. This work comes out of the American 'culture wars' and associated academic debates over identity and sexuality, and leads into the discourse of gender performance and queer theory, both of which contain powerful deconstructions of the grotesque sexual stereotypes that pervade heterosexism.

The Politics of Gender Performance: Butler

From Marilyn Monroe to Madonna, from Frank Sinatra to the Spice Girls, popular culture is held in thrall to the lures of sexuality. Culturally, it is as if we are trapped in the very 'look' of sex, enticed by the codes of gender. The self, as the radical American feminist Judith Butler has argued, is always 'dressing up' for sex, or putting on a performance of gender, a performance in which selves are constituted and authenticated. It has been Butler's fate to be associated with a variety of radical feminist projects, from lesbian theory to the new queer discourses. Her innovative theoretical exploration of the conditions of gender construction and sexual performance has brought together diverse currents of critical theory, and her writings are strongly indebted to the perspectives elaborated by such French theorists as Foucault, Lacan and Kristeva. She is the author of several feminist tracts, of which *Gender Trouble* (1990) is justly the most celebrated.

In *Gender Trouble* Butler seeks to lay bare the performative, constructed nature of gender identities. She is out to expose the violence and tautology of the notion of 'core gender identity', the view of women and men as two distinct, fixed selves. She believes that the traditional conception of antithetical gender identities profoundly limits our sexual repertoires, and crushes the psychic, emotional, intimate and social possibilities for expression of the self. This is an issue of considerable interest, and Butler's proposals for radical feminist theory and practice are bold. No feminist has ever made the equation between performance, gender identity and sexual power quite so explicit. Soft porn, heterosexual desire – that is Butler's image of the stereotypical gender relation enacted between men and women. Critically surveying assumed patterns of heterosexuality and homosexuality, she analyses with great flair the cultural possibilities and inhibitions affecting the gender identities we fashion in the making of the self.

In the opening chapter of *Gender Trouble*, Butler proceeds by calling into question the ways in which feminism has constructed itself as an identity-based theory. She problematizes, in effect, the very notion of a coherent feminine sense of self. Recognizing that the specification of a unitary subject identity has facilitated feminist theory and politics in various ways, she nonetheless argues that the time has come to break with identity politics. This is necessary, in part, because of the devastating critiques of identity-based feminism delivered in recent years by women of colour and postcolonial critics; the charge here is that the appeal to woman made in the name of feminism has inevitably excluded some women, especially black and Third World women. But it is also due to key conceptual instabilities that have plagued the idea of gender identity in feminist discussions of the self. Feminists have for the most part, according to Butler, assumed a pre-established sexed body, a body to which the field of gender construction (itself fraught with conflict and contradiction) somehow magically connects. The French feminist Simone de Beauvoir's writings are examined in this context by Butler, specifically her claim that gender is socially constructed. 'One is not born a woman, but rather one becomes one', as de Beauvoir famously put this. For Butler, the problem with de Beauvoir's thesis concerning the social construction of gender is that it uncritically assumes that the fabrication of identity automatically connects to an already sexed body. That is to say, de Beauvoir's feminism, ironically, reaffirms the ties between gender and anatomy. There are sexed bodies (female and

male), to which the social construction of sex adds antithetical gendered selves (women and men). But why, as Butler
asks, do we seek to limit the social construction of gender to
either the male or the female body? Might such constructions
not cross and tangle? Can one not identify across the geography, particularly the in-between spaces, of gender? And
who, ultimately, decides the mix of heterosexual and homosexual versions of the self in the constitution of the sexed
body?

These are some of the issues raised by Butler's elaboration
of a performative theory of gender and the self. Following
Foucault, Butler calls the production of self and gender a
'discursive effect'. That is to say, the identity categories at the
centre of women's and men's lives are fashioned through our
involvement with, and subjection to, cultural and linguistic
codes. Rather than understand the self in terms of inner
desires, psychological capacities or emotional needs, Butler
says that the self is produced in the act of performing sexuality, doing gender and enacting desires. There is for Butler 'no
doer behind the deed'; people only come to see themselves as
possessing inner lives and psychological identities through a
set of repeated gender performances. Butler's performative
self can thus be described as a kind of radical Foucaultianism,
in which performances on the outside congeal over time to
create an illusion of self on the inside. Our performances of
self are fashioned after the cultural representations of masculinity and femininity that we see all around us in modern
society; through imitation we perform the self in such a
manner as to weave together sexuality, gender, eroticism, sex
and desire. Enacted sexualities and performed genders,
according to Butler, encode highly regulated forms of power,
domination and social norms. She emphasizes how dominant
heterosexual relations regulate practices of gender, and profoundly limit performed identities of sexuality.

There are many ways in which we might identify the
making of gender norms in performances of heterosexual
culture. Consider, for instance, the mimetic aspects of the
marriage ceremony in modern society. The marriage ceremony, largely irrespective of the religious commitments of the
parties involved, is today increasingly rendered a cultural
space for conspicuous consumption, the display of wealth, an

exhibition of style, fashion and aesthetic value. The bride and groom act out roles that mix together love, intimacy, gender and sex. Interestingly, society pages in newspapers and magazines devote considerable coverage to the bridal wedding dress, particularly for weddings of the wealthy and famous. No detail is spared in discussing the bride's dress as regards neckline, headpiece, veil, as well as bouquet. In fact, one might well argue that it is through the display of the dress, and the gender performance this necessarily entails, that the woman is actually constituted as a 'bride'. But just as self and gender interlock in ceremonial performances, so too does the self for Butler stylize and fashion sexuality through repeated gender performances in day-to-day life. If the terrain of self-identity is one of our main cultural anxieties today, Butler boldly maps our daily performative labours in linking sex and gender – from the production of the body beautiful and fit self to the professional and working self.

Every performance of identity is also always potentially disruptive or disturbing, and it is in this context that Butler seeks to give some specific political weight to her feminist analysis. Perhaps not surprisingly for a feminist writing in the 1990s, in which the radical potential of institutional politics was regarded as in decline, Butler identifies sub-cultural sites of politics – specifically 'drag' and 'gender bending' – as transgressive of the notion of a true gender identity.

> In imitating gender, drag implicitly reveals the imitative structure of gender itself – as well as its contingency. Indeed, part of the pleasure, the giddiness of the performance is in the recognition of a radical contingency in the relation between sex and gender in the face of cultural configurations of causal unities that are regularly assumed to be natural and necessary. (*Gender Trouble*, London: Routledge, 1990, pp. 137–8)

What are modern men and women doing, Butler seems to be asking, imagining that sex and gender automatically fit together? If only we could learn more artful performances of self – based upon parody and mimicry – then we might well reach a deeper appreciation of how fearful and destructive our mundane fusion of sex and gender has been. Yet, if it is not obvious to the reader how gender parody might release mass opinion from the 'radical contingency' of sex and gender, it is surely striking how such an approach trades on marginality and the marginal in establishing its radical political credentials. After all, the celebration of gay parody or lesbian mimicry seems a reasonably safe bet for laying down a supposedly radical critique of the 'fixed gender identities' of the cultural mainstream. As some of Butler's critics suggest, her politics is one that trades on radical chic, advocating the kind of progressive attitudes which play relentlessly to her own audience (principally academe and the avant-garde), while all the time hypocritically denouncing the terrors of 'elitism'.

Butler's writings are in some ways reminiscent of those of Erving Goffman, whose sociological reflections on the skilled performances of social actors were discussed in chapter 1. Like Goffman, Butler shifts the terms of debate over the self from those of personal motives and biographical dispositions to social doing and human action. Unlike Goffman, however, Butler's anti-humanist feminist politics disconnects performances of doing from the self altogether. Let me be very clear about the implications of this criticism, since the relationship between performance and the self has been clumsily dealt with by some of Butler's followers. Now, the self is clearly not some kind of mini-agent, moving behind or determining various role performances. Performances, as Goffman aptly demonstrates, are fundamental to the agency of the self as well as the presentation of agency to other social agents. Butler, however, remains undistracted by such finer conceptual linkages of self, agency and performance. Notwithstanding drawing from the psychoanalytic perspectives of Lacan and Kristeva, there is an awkwardness to Butler's treatment of the passions and desires of the self. Her work shows little feel for the emotional dynamics of human relationships, and she clearly prefers the post-structuralist terrain of discourse to any trace of desire – a trait also shared by Foucault. The difficulty here is not that Butler does away with traditional sociological and philosophical conceptions of the self – that much is true of most of the theories I discuss in this book, from psychoanalysis to postmodernism. Rather, in her uncritical adoption of Foucault, Butler denounces not only identity but also the self-constituting elements of identification. (This limitation has been corrected in some of Butler's subsequent work, which is more psychoanalytic in orientation, though, interestingly, her recent work has been less influential in current feminist debate.) We may agree that a self's social existence is firmly rooted in situated performances; but an exploration of the psychic identifications underlying perform-ance suggests there are affective, less behavioural patternings; in short, desires that evolve into a mystery beyond action and doing.

Butler's own political sympathies are distinctly pluralistic, and in the final chapters of *Gender Trouble* she repeatedly speaks up for the transgressive, the wild, the untamed and the bizarre. The making of gender trouble, according to Butler, involves complex stratifications and mobilities of power and gender, an uncertain sexuality based on transgres-sive expectations and the desire to shock. The drag queen, the macho gay, the femme lesbian: all such conspicuous performances problematize sex and give the slip to the coer-cive power of heterosexuality and patriarchal discourses. However, each reference Butler makes to disturbance, disrup-tion or transgression of heterosexuality gains its rhetorical force only by invoking the spectre of normal or routine per-formances of sex in social relations. Butler seems to think this is how it is with most of us, and to this extent her work grievously underestimates the various ways in which people refuse, or dis-identify with, the norms and identities of con-ventional society. Postmodern theory is highly relevant to grasping the limits of Butler's division of gender into main-stream and transgressive, as it teaches us to be wary of dichotomy. Drag has been popular with both mainstream and alternative audiences; it would, for instance, be hard to see how a film such as *Priscilla: Queen of the Desert* might get itself included on the transgressive gender map. There would seem to be little room for ambivalence and uncertainty in Butler's picturing of our sexual world, and it is not evident that her approach can grasp the richly varied ways in which individuals imagine their sexual lives (Butler's emphasis on performance tends to limit analytical attention to imagina-tion), nor the manner in which self-identity and personal worth are evaluated.

Notwithstanding these criticisms, Butler's feminism is theoretically dense and disarming. Her work has helped set a tone for other critical mappings of self and sexuality, particularly in queer theory – which we will now turn to examine.

Queer Theory: Contesting Self, Defying Gender

The affirmation of self-identity can sometimes be as much limiting as freeing. Controversies over the personal and cultural problems involved in identity politics, especially in respect of asserting a common identity and community, have frequently plagued those committed to progressive sexual politics. The dilemma is primarily one of how to redress social exclusion and political oppression by creating a new sense of self, solidarity and community while avoiding the confinement of fixed identities and categories. Most of us, most of the time, make sense of identity by telling stories about our experience, shared understanding, sense of communal belonging and so forth. We want the interrelationship between personal and cultural life to be open-ended in this complex and pluralistic world; we seek to avoid simple generalizations about our identity, and none of us wants our experience coded as stereotype. A preoccupation with the relation between personal identity and social difference has been increasingly central to sexual politics over the last few decades, especially as developed by the lesbian and gay movement and also in queer theory and politics. The core challenge for the self, as defined by such standpoints, is to find some balance between the need for identity and the recognition of cultural diversity and social difference. In the remainder of this chapter. I shall chart some of these changes in the intimate texture of social life, paying special attention to conceptions of the self that have arisen from contemporary sexual politics. Contemporary feminist and gay studies in particular have developed powerful ideas about the historical formation of sexual identities, with the social impact of the science of sexuality a key theme. This research represents, in many respects, an alternative history of the self and sexual identity, and it is worth briefly noting some of the more salient aspects of such perspectives on sexual identity and the self.

There are various ways of denoting sexual orientation. At various historical points, in various cultures, the terms 'homosexual', 'gay', 'lesbian' and 'queer' have been deployed to refer to same-sex sexual desires and practices. The etymological evolution of 'homosexual' is especially interesting in this context. The word 'homosexual' was coined in 1868 by the sex reformer Karl Kertbeny; it was taken up by a Swiss medical practitioner, Karoly Maria Benkert, the following year. Yet it was not until the end of the nineteenth century that the word became commonly used in English, and indeed a public culture involving core distinctions between homosexuality and heterosexuality as distinctive identities did not fully emerge until some point in the 1920s or 1930s. Prior to this homosexuality was – for the most part – thought of as a particular kind of behaviour; the law punished illegal activity (sodomy), not deviant identity. The slow filtering through of the medical/expert term 'homosexual' into public discourse and common culture changed all this, and is a good example of the intrusion of expert knowledge into the fabric of daily life that I have emphasized in preceding chapters. For it was in and through this invasion of social scientific knowledge that homosexuality came, in time, to be established as a unique identity, a specific psychological disposition, a particular sense of self, and thus as separated or marked off from the heterosexual mainstream. This in turn opened a path to the coercive idea that psychological health depends upon a normalized sense of personal identity, something to which homosexuality was from the beginning excluded in the view of the medical establishment. For homosexuality, in the majority of medical discourses, was treated as a pathology. But it also opened a path for the ongoing interrogation of identity – in this context, a problematization of the idea that homosexuals have a specific sexual nature and sense of self. *Coming Out* (1977), by the gay studies theorist Jeffrey Weeks, accounts for homosexual identity as just such a cross between social and historical event on the one hand and the absorption of social scientific ideas governing sexuality by the wider public on the other. In charting the role of science, especially sexology, in the historical making of a specific homosexual

identity, Weeks tells a compelling story of how these historical forces have shaped identity-based gay liberation in both
progressive and constraining ways.

Throughout the 1960s and 1970s the rise of gay liberation
in many Western countries was closely associated with an
ongoing interrogation of dominant conceptions of sexuality,
self and identity. Some gay writers argued that homosexuality
was psychologically and socially the equal of heterosexuality;
this standpoint, in one stroke, embraced all in the mainstream
who viewed the homosexual as a distinct type of person, but
with the crucial inversion that homosexuality was now cast
as just as morally worthy as heterosexuality. According to
this approach, which in one version or another was extensively adopted in the gay movement, the notion of a distinctive sense of personal and sexual identity should be deployed
to defend gays against the homophobia of the wider culture,
and thus to advance gay rights.

There are a number of important criticisms of the political
radicalism of gay liberation. I shall note in passing only those
that directly relate to the topic of the self. It is sometimes
argued, particularly by postmodern sexual theorists, that gay
liberation rode roughshod over race, ethnic and class differences. There is some accuracy to this charge, since the desire
to legislate an affirmative gay identity was often pursued at
the cost of awareness of wider social issues – especially igno-
rance of the emotional damage that other social and historical
forces have had upon the self. However, this argument can
be overstressed; there is always a danger of oversimplification
when discussing the gay movement as a unified entity, and in
fact many gay activists shared a strong political commitment
to other issues of discrimination (such as the Black and union
movements). Perhaps more importantly, and no doubt ironically, the gay liberation movement has been criticized by
many for reinforcing the divide between homosexual and
heterosexual cultures, positing essentialist identities, and
carving the world into majority and minority experience.

In time, the identity framework of the gay movement gave
way to a different sort of politics concerned with sexual
identities, preferences and activities, one connected with the
new social theories of post-structuralism and postmodernism.
In the late 1980s and 1990s the term 'queer' was used by

theorists and activists alike to attack identity politics, to interrogate sexuality and decentre the self, and to construct alternative political geographies for the heterosexual/homosexual
divide that shapes our communities and cultures. Queer
theory represents a sexual politics sensitive to our new era of
transnational capital, globalized technology and postmodern
culture. The social and historical forces influencing the shift
from identity to queer politics are located in the fragmentation of social identities and political alignments associated
with globalization. Queer politics is pluralistic, multidimen-
sional and open-ended, especially at the level of addressing
experience of the self and sexuality.

The writings of Diana Fuss are important in this context.
Reflecting upon the widespread discontent with identity
politics in the 1980s, Fuss developed an influential critique
of the ways in which gay and lesbian liberation discourses
unwittingly reinforced heterosexual norms; her critique,
in turn, shaped the politics of subversion advocated by
queer theorists. Describing configurations of sex, gender and
sexuality in terms of our culture's obsession with notions of
sameness and difference, Fuss contended that the opposition
between homosexuality and heterosexuality reinforced the
social imperative to divide the world between norm and
pathology, inclusion and exclusion, identity and otherness.
The hetero/homosexual logic of identity is one premised
on difference. Such forms of sexual orientation, however,
are in fact constantly crossing into each other. It is only
through psychological exclusion and repression that homosexuality is rendered subordinate to heterosexuality. Part
of the problem here, according to Fuss, is that we are lost
in identity, its logic and categories. Questioning identity
categories, Fuss asks:

> Is politics based on identity, or is identity based on politics?
> Is identity a natural, political, historical, psychical, or linguis-
> tic construct? What implications does the deconstruction of
> 'identity' have for those who espouse an identity politics? Can
> feminist, gay, or lesbian subjects afford to dispense with the
> notion of unified, stable identities or must we begin to base
> our politics on something other than identity? What, in other
> words, is the politics of 'identity politics'? (Diana Fuss, *Essen-
> tially Speaking*, New York: Routledge, 1989, p. 100)

Fuss asks us, in effect, to consider what our lives might be like without the anxious grip of identity categories. She questions what the self can do without, a challenge taken up and developed in queer theory and politics in the 1990s.

The best-known and most influential author associated with the queer critique of feminist theorizing is Eve Kosofsky Sedgwick, routinely described as 'the mother of queer theory'. A professor of English with an uncanny gift for grappling with the sexual politics of language, Sedgwick stresses the experiential significance of discourses on homosexuality not only for the self and identity, but also for the production and distribution of knowledge in the wider society. In her most important book, *The Epistemology of the Closet* (1991), Sedgwick describes the hetero/homosexual opposition as our culture's 'master term', a term that to its core structures not only self, identity and sexuality, but also social conventions, modes of thought and cultural knowledge. The normative regulations and sanctions governing homosexuality have never applied, and never will, to gays and lesbians alone; rather, they cut to the heart of heterosexual identity, which maintains itself in opposition to homosexual experience. But what is repressed returns. Heterosexuality and homosexuality are intimately, hysterically intertwined; homosexual identifications, for Sedgwick as for Butler, are contained within heterosexual relationships, just as heterosexuality is gathered up and transfigured in gay and lesbian relationships.

Sedgwick has perhaps done more to interrogate the political limits of self, identity and sexuality than any other scholar associated with contemporary gay and lesbian studies. Her version of queer theory is out to demonstrate that homosexuality is integral to the culture of heterosexuality which hysterically repudiates same-sex desire. Not surprisingly, given her predilection for language as at the centre of social life, Sedgwick worries away at the cluster of key words that betray the dreads of heterosexist culture. Thus 'the closet' turns out to ground knowledge of sexuality and gender in ways that pathologize. Bluntly put, Sedgwick argues that 'the closet' – as representation, metaphor, desire, fantasy – is installed at the heart of both homosexual and heterosexual identity, experience and definition. Consider, for example, the experience of coming out. Coming-out stories have long been a common part of gay experience. 'It's OK to be gay': this is one of the better-known slogans promoted by the gay and lesbian movement to assist young people negotiating the difficulties of coming to terms with their homosexuality. Yet for the most part, asserts Sedgwick, coming-out stories have the capacity to disturb and damage dominant conceptions of sexuality. Because of the erotic energy and anxious fear associated with the closet and coming out, we can never know the truth about the self, sexuality or gender. The closet is the underside of 'normal sexuality', always threatening to open or be opened.

The political implications of such an assault on identity categories, in the recent history of queer theory at least, are highly ambiguous. In the work of Fuss, Sedgwick and others, legitimating forms of cultural identity as something coherent, unified or fixed are progressively called into question by a subversive critique that interrogates the oppressive fusing of sex, gender and sexuality at the level of the self. As a kind of anti-identity politics, then, queer theory advocates and celebrates a coalition of alternative, subversive and transgressive sexual identities. Queer politics embraces not only lesbian, gay and bisexual identities, but also fetishists, sadists, drag queens, transsexuals, butches and gender benders. The mobilization of identities as queer is potentially indeterminate, as the assessment of queerness depends on a self-identification with forms of sexuality that question or subvert 'the normal' within patriarchal power relations. Like much postmodernist culture, queer theory and politics is unashamedly open-ended, plural and multiple; the transgression of sexual norms is the key that defines queerness. But how transgression constitutes a progressive politics is not altogether clear. Jeffrey Weeks makes this criticism well:

> In the long perspectives of history, queer politics may well prove an ephemeral ripple rather than a refreshing wave. Queer politics has all the defects of a transgressive style, elevating confrontation over the content of alternatives.
>
> Although it seeks to deconstruct old rigidities, it creates new boundaries; although it is deliberately transgressive, it enacts dissidence through the adoption of a descriptive label which many lesbians and gays find offensive, often seeking

enemies within as much as enemies without. (Jeffrey Weeks, *Invented Moralities*, Cambridge: Polity, 1995, p. 115)

Much like Butler's notion of subversive performance, the slant towards transgression in queer theory is perhaps geared more towards fashion than the fine detail of concrete political transformation.

It is against this backdrop that some commentators have suggested that queer theory is unable to provide a progressive basis for politics. The emphasis upon literary deconstruction in queer theorizing is, for some critics, intellectually interesting but politically shallow; the whole style of queer theory, with its relentless droning of sexual transgression, is said to be apolitical, with little analytical concern for the realities of social institutions, economic development or the policies of government. In postmodern culture, the language of transgression is sometimes only an inch away from anti-political irrationalism – or so some argue. Others, however, welcome queer theory's dismantling of social science and literary criticism as distinct fields of study, and see in the queer critique of identity a radical revaluation not only of self-experience and social relationships, but also of knowledge and politics. Indeed, as Patricia Clough has argued, the style of queer theoretical interrogations of the self, identity and sexuality suggests that style itself is political, always overdetermined with cultural assumptions and sexual ideologies. In particular, the style of mainstream social science, with its patriarchal longing for certitude, structure and order, is rendered dubious in this respect.

Similar doubts hang over the question of the self in queer theory. Is queer theory's ongoing interrogation of selfhood radical or reactionary? Certainly, the focus of queer theory upon, say, transvestite performance or gender-corrective surgery dramatizes the incoherence of our culture's obsession with stable selves, identities, sexualities and genders. But it is far from obvious that, in its relentless debunking of the self and identity politics, queer theory can provide any psychological analysis of self. It is one thing to decentre or deconstruct the autonomous, rational, masculinist self of Enlightenment culture; yet it is quite another to imagine that self as a category can be conveniently done away with altogether. The critique of identity I have described in the foregoing pages, from Butler to Sedgwick, does not, in my opinion, attempt to transcend the realm of individuality and the self in such a manner. It remains the case, however, that the exuberance and idealism of queer theory, however intellectually invigorating the call to sexual transgression might be, does underestimate the considerable personal and emotional difficulties involved in cultural change and political transformation.

5
The Postmodern Self

A highly important set of changes occurring today, to which I have so far referred only in passing, concerns the altered economic and social context of work, employment and unemployment and its relation to personal life. The emergence of new forms of industrial (or post-industrial) work, and their associated impact upon the self, can be identified in various ways. At an economic level, jobs in the industrial sector have been disappearing over the last few decades, while jobs in the service industry and communications sector have rapidly expanded. Moreover, in our speed-driven information age, global capitalism has substituted more flexible forms of work (short-term, contract, unstable) for employment in the classic sense (full-time, long-term, benefits guaranteed). At a personal level it appears increasingly evident that the shift to temporary, part-time, flexible employment is unnerving, risk-laden and conflictual. People entering the workforce today not only face the prospect of a drastically shortened working life, but might also expect to change jobs as well as their skill base several times. Transposed to the realm of the self and self-identity, the disorientating effects of the new capitalism means there is little stable ground for an individual to lodge an anchor. 'Keep moving and don't commit yourself' is perhaps the moral to be drawn from today's hi-tech global economy.

If downsizing, flexibility and job insecurity have become the mark of our times, how might these changes affect people's emotional lives? How do such economic changes impinge upon the self? And how can long-term personal goals – that is, the self as a project – be pursued in a world devoted to the short term? Richard Sennett, one of the leaders of American sociology, has shown just how difficult the imperatives of flexibility and risk-taking can be in the world of work. He has also shown how damaging an economy without long-term commitments or larger meaning can be for self-identity and the self. *The Corrosion of Character* is Sennett's sociological study of how global capitalism frustrates the attempts of men and women to achieve a mature and stable sense of self. His argument, bluntly put, is that we have moved from a work world of rigid, hierarchical organizations, in which self-discipline shaped the durability of the self, to a brave new economy of corporate re-engineering, innovation and risk, in which the fragmented or dislocated nature of self-experience moves to the fore.

At the heart of Sennett's book is the story of Rico, a materially successful businessman, in the top 5 per cent of the wage scale, but who feels dissatisfied with his high-pressured lifestyle. What most surprises Sennett about Rico is the degree to which his personal sense of identity is shaped by the dictates of work. For, after graduating from university and marrying a fellow student, Rico changed jobs four times after reaching the top of his profession – with each move carrying complicated emotional disturbances for himself and his family. Rico works in the hi-tech electronics industry; it is a world that involves him in continual networking, online short communications, flexible contracts and the like. In discussion with Sennett, Rico confesses to feeling emotionally adrift and vulnerable; he worries that his highly demanding job leads him to neglect his wife and children; he worries about the weak ties that define his few friendships; he worries, above all, about a lack of ethical discipline, fearing the superficial morality that defines his life. Prosperous as he is, Rico is a man whose life is dominated by the imperatives of the money market; the more he tries to adjust to the dynamic pressures of the global market, the more he feels he is losing control of his purpose in life and his sense of self.

When people are inserted into a world of detachment and superficial cooperativeness, of weak ties and interchangeable relationships, and when all this is shaped by the pursuit of risk-taking and self-reinvention, the power of traditional social norms and cultural traditions begins to diminish. This can be potentially liberating: the self finds the potential to define itself anew and create fluid and innovative social relationships. But there is also something deeply unsettling. For a self that is constituted entirely through episodes and fragments has little to hold itself together in emotional terms; and it is this drift of character, of corrosion of the self, that Sennett fixes his attention firmly upon. According to Sennett, as the coherent life narrative breaks down, so does the symbolic texture of the self. In contemporary social conditions durable selfhood is replaced by a kind of supermarket identity – an assemblage of scraps, random desires, chance encounters, the accidental and the fleeting. Moreover, as Sennett notes, this suits the requirements of dynamic global capitalism: 'A pliant self, a collage of fragments unceasing in its becoming, ever open to the new experience – these are just the psychological conditions suited to the short-term work experience, flexible institutions, and constant risk-taking' (Sennett, *The Corrosion of Character*, New York: Norton, 1998, p. 133). According to Sennett, the flexible regime of the new capitalism – with its instant global transfers of money, its hi-tech cultural production, and its radical restructuring of the labour market – begets a character structure geared towards the superficial, the fleeting and the fragmented. 'In the flexible, fragmented present', he writes, 'it may seem possible only to create coherent narratives about what has been, and no longer possible to create predictive narratives about what will be' (ibid.: 135).

To speak of the self in terms of fragments, flux and an endless process of self-creation is to adopt a highly contemporary – sometimes labelled 'postmodern' – slant on identity. Postmodernism, which frames our discussion of the self in this final chapter, has been understood as a new social condition in which corporate capitalism and consumer lifestyles are dominant, new technological transformations become pervasive at the level of daily life, and the grand objectives of the Enlightenment (including Truth, Justice, Reason and Equality) dissolve or become irrelevant in a world shaped by mass popular culture. More on the precise implications and ramifications of postmodernism shortly. At this point, I want simply to note that Sennett's emphasis on the fragmentation, dislocation and decomposition of identity and everyday working life fits very well with some of the core preoccupations of postmodern theory. He sees the part played by information technology in the restructuring of global capitalism as having very profound consequences for self-identity. Such consequences are likely to be negative and destructive for the self, according to Sennett. Certainly, he thinks we should be wary of the 'digital divide' and the arrival of new forms of social power based on media technology, again because strong objections can be brought against the harmful impact such technologies have upon local communities, familial relationships and personal identity.

Let us now contrast Sennett's rather gloomy portrait of the self with the views of another contemporary American sociologist, Sherry Turkle. Turkle's interest is also in identity and the self. Unlike Sennett, however, Turkle takes her cue, not from the world of work, but rather cyberspace and the Internet. In *Life on the Screen* (New York: Weidenfeld and Nicolson, 1995) she sets out to explore the mysteries of relationships forged on the Internet, giving special attention to the self. Her book examines the self by focusing upon Internet relay chat rooms and text-based virtual reality sites that allow people to connect to the same place at the same time. What especially interests her is the manner in which individuals experiment online with their sense of self; the ways in which people invent themselves as they go along, exploring, constructing and reconstructing their identities. Turkle views such technological developments in a positive fashion; she thinks new communication technology is potentially liberating for the self, and argues that the Internet offers a powerful corrective to old-fashioned cultural anxiety about the corrosive effects of the mass media.

One of the more intriguing case studies in *Life on the Screen* concerns virtual sex. The interesting thing about 'netsex', says Turkle, is that anything goes. People can easily change their genders, sexual orientations, personalities, race, ethnicity, class, status – in short, the individual can devise a net-self that outstrips the real self. According to Turkle, cybersex is intrinsically fragmentary and episodic – which is, surely, part of its appeal. With the press of a button, one can move from flirtation to cross-dressing, from fetishism to sadomasochism. Turkle provides an interesting example of a young man who discovers that his girlfriend habitually identities herself as a man and has cybersex with female characters in chat rooms. At first the man is not sure what to make of this. After all, he muses, there are only words at stake. But are there? As Turkle points out, cybersex raises the question of what is at the heart of identity and the self. The fact that the physical body has been factored out of the equation, she argues, only makes an assessment of the self more troubling. Ultimately she finds this liberating in the sense that self-identity can now be fashioned free from the stain of traditional social markers, such as class, race and gender. The restructuring of the self via simulation, according to Turkle, permits experimentation with alternative identities and different imaginings. Liberation here consists in the fact that no representation of the self is more authentic or deeper than the next; it is the trying on of different identities which is freeing.

Like Sennett, Turkle tries to assess the contemporary state of the self through reference to the ideas of postmodernism. The cultural impact of the Internet is important in this connection, as cyberspace for Turkle brings the philosophical ideas of postmodernists down to earth. Today's culture, she says, is increasingly experienced as a collection of fragments and episodes. To live in the postmodern world, according to Turkle, is to live a discontinuous, fractured, episodic, consequences-avoiding life. Her argument is that the Internet is the socio-technical field which best expresses these postmodern tendencies, a field in which people explore and develop new selves.

A comparison of the work of Sennett and Turkle highlights alternative tendencies that sit side by side in recent postmodern conceptualizations of the self. On the one hand, there is recognition that global culture reshapes the self in powerful, and sometimes disturbing and frightening, ways. Accompanying this, there is an attempt to understand the reconstitution of the self under cultural conditions of fragmentation, dislocation and dispersal. On the other hand, there is the desire to celebrate the potentialities of postmodern identity, to assess the liberating possibilities opened for the self, self-identity and subjectivity. In this final chapter I shall look at the ways in which our understanding of the self alters when identity is viewed through the lens of these strands of postmodernist theory.

All that is Modern Melts into Postmodern?

Mention the term 'postmodern' and it often brings a knee-jerk reaction of discomfort. What is it with postmodernism? Why does the notion provoke anxiety? For many people, the writings of postmodernists are jargon-ridden, shot through with obscure terms and ideas. What is the difference between the mafia and the postmodernists? The mafia makes you an offer you can't refuse; the postmodernists make you one you can't understand! While there may be some merit to this viewpoint, it is equally true that the debate about postmodernism has largely been treated as a purely academic affair – as something for English or philosophy departments to busy themselves with. As a consequence, the personal and subjective significance of this debate has often been obscured. However, the intellectual controversies surrounding postmodernism arise from an altered institutional context. At the current time we are witnessing profound social transformations. The rise of transnational corporations and the expansion of the international economy; the proliferation of global forms of communication; major changes in patterns of the production and consumption of goods and services; global population movements; the techno-industrialization of war and associated transformations in military activity; the emergence of identity politics, of regional and ethnic conflicts over difference and cultural particularity; the dominance of the mass media and communication technologies in daily life: these transformations amount to a reconstitution of the fabric of our contemporary social, cultural and political condition.

Pointing to these social transformations, some social theorists argue that we are at the end of the era of modernity – an era dominated by industrial capitalism. 'All that is solid melts into air', as Karl Marx famously said of the powers of capitalism to break apart traditional forms of social life. Today, by contrast, there are few solids to melt. According to some, the oppressive, repetitive grind of industrial labour has been left behind for good – at least in the West, if not in the Third World. Industrialization is replaced by post-industrial technology, the era of the computer microchip. Here we might recall Sennett's portrait of Rico, a man of whom it might be said that post-industrial technology came to invade the inner fabric of his life and sense of self. It came to invade his life in the sense that the flexibility and ruthless risk-taking that his work demanded of him entered into a disturbing contradiction with his personal commitments and family responsibilities. In time Rico came to feel cut off, disconnected and dislocated, from both his public and his personal commitments. For many commentators seeking to come to grips with these altered personal and public contexts, it is assumed that we live in a world that is very different from the recent past, a world that is complex and novel, enticing and threatening. In this new social condition, Marx's dictum is replaced by a new catch-cry: 'All that is modern melts into postmodern.'

It is not my intention to develop in what follows another definition of postmodernism. Rather, I want to stress that however one defines the new times in which we are living – 'postmodernity', 'post-industrial society', 'the end of history', 'information society', 'consumer society' – there is an increasing and constructive emphasis in contemporary social research on analysing the changing dispositions, attitudes, feelings and desires that people are experiencing in relation to themselves, other people and the wider world. The series of global transitions relating to information technology, computerization and the wholesale commodification of everyday life, in particular, entangles the self in the exhilarating and threatening potentialities of postmodernity as a whole. The expansion of communication systems across the globe, coupled with a dramatic acceleration in the turmoil and flux of personal and cultural life arising from intensified capitalist competition, provide the backdrop for retracing the constitution of the self, selfhood and individual subjectivity.

Of the various states of mind that define the core contours of postmodern selfhood, there are three that are especially prominent in the literature. First, there is an emphasis upon fragmentation. The postmodernist critique suggests that the contemporary self is so fragmented, multiple and dispersed that the symbolic consistency and narrative texture of experience disintegrates. In a world invaded by new technologies and saturated with flashy commodities, the self loses its consistency, and becomes brittle, broken or shattered. Second, the flickering media surfaces of postmodern culture are, according to this view, mirrored internally, so that a narcissistic preoccupation with appearance, image and style dominates the regulation of the self. This is a world that puts a premium on appearance, a world of spin doctors, public relations experts and self-help guides. The self, in this context, can easily lose its anchorage, becoming self-absorbed and cut off from wider social ties. Third, there is a new centrality accorded to fantasy and phantasmagoria on the personal and social levels, so that the dream, hallucination and madness take on an added importance at the expense of common stocks of knowledge or rationality. In conditions of postmodernity, in the West at any rate, people seem to be experiencing a mixture of confusion, dispersal and disillusionment on the one hand, and excitement, desire and the possibility for personal development on the other. The image of postmodernity presented above – with its shimmering media surfaces, its cult of hi-tech, and its pervasive globalization – resonates with a state of mind split between the enticing excitement of casino capitalism and the terrifying spectre of nuclear catastrophe.

In chapter 2, I mentioned that the theory of the self developed by the French psychoanalyst Jacques Lacan has been influential in recent discussions of contemporary culture. Some of the most provocative descriptions of postmodern selfhood have been developed with reference to Lacanian theory, particularly in terms of imagination, desire and representation. In this sort of analysis Lacan's stress on mirrored images is taken to evoke central characteristics of the contemporary age, especially the splintering, surface aspects of current selfhood. Discussion of the postmodern condition is, in fact, often conducted with specific reference to Lacan's notion of the 'mirror stage'. According to Lacan, fragmentation, loss and mourning are at the heart of the psyche; and this means that, no matter how hard individuals try to find various emotional substitutes for loss, a profound sense of emptiness always marks the self. The ego, Lacan says, blinds the self to such loss; the ego covers over the fragmentation of the psyche through narcissistic illusions of perfection and completeness. Through immersion in the realm of images and representations, the ego is built upon various narcissistic identifications that defend against the painful and unsettling turbulence of the unconscious. The individual captivated by its mirror image, or the self treating other people as mirror to its own wants and desires: these are instances of imaginary misrecognition, a distortion through which the ego seeks to fill in the gap of emptiness, loss and longing at the level of unconscious desire.

Lacan's account of the ego as a distorting trap – a narcissistic mirage which papers over the fracturing and fragmentation of the psyche – has been invoked by many commentators to theorize the postmodern condition. Cultural analysts influenced by Lacan seek to unearth the symbolic forms and cultural fictions used by individuals in conditions of postmodernity to define their narcissistic identifications, to integrate their torn selves, and to shape identities (however brittle) distinct from their precarious personal subjectivity. From this standpoint, the glittering surfaces and dazzling images of postmodern culture come to be mirrored internally, taken inside the mind to make something of identity. As there is little substance or depth to postmodern culture, however, these internalized, flattened images permit the self to construct only a superficial or fleeting sense of identity. The flickering image of the video screen has replaced the warm conviviality of familial relationships as the linchpin of internalization for the self – or so some theorists suggest. The postmodern self, created upon fleeting narcissistic images, is a transient identity with precious little in the way of deeper affective ties or emotional roots.

Many analysts agree that fragmentation, dislocation and contradiction are key characteristics of postmodernity that are mirrored internally at the level of the self. Not all, however, would accept the Lacanian stress on loss, emptiness and despair. According to an alternative standpoint, the sense of cultural fragmentation that is emblematic of postmodernity lies at the core of a particular kind of schizophrenic experience which is increasingly prevalent today. Rather than lament this situation, authors aligned with this theoretical position argue, perhaps ironically and no doubt a little naively, that psychosis is something to be celebrated; against the oppressive, male-dominated, bureaucratic world of rationality and rational thinking, schizophrenia is viewed as genuinely creative, affirmative and potentially liberating. The French philosophers Gilles Deleuze (1925–95) and Felix Guattari (1930–92) have expressed this idea in its most radical form in their book *Anti-Oedipus: Capitalism and Schizophrenia* (1977), contending that the schizophrenic is revolutionary. Deleuze and Guattari regard any notion of the self that posits a unitary structure as tyrannical. Their position, by contrast, celebrates fragmentation, multiplicity and discontinuity. They argue for the radical political potential of schizophrenia, for a break-up of our linear and bureaucratic world through randomness, decentring and disconnected identities. Given the extreme nature of Deleuze and Guattari's claims regarding psychosis, the historical context of *Anti-Oedipus* should be mentioned here. The book became hugely popular in the wake of May 1968, when French students and workers rose up against the state and, for a brief moment at least, almost brought down the de Gaulle government. These student and labour protests were widely supported by the general public, and indeed the political counterculture of the time raised important and lasting issues concerning the ideology of subversion, the politics of daily life and sexual politics. It was against this backdrop that Deleuze and Guattari's claim that the schizophrenic is a 'hero of desire' gained some level of political appeal.

With the passing of the revolts of May 1968, as well as the emergence of a pessimistic sense that many people were both afraid of and anxious about political change and social revolt, the shortcomings of Deleuze and Guartarri's supposedly radical political agenda have become plain. Criticisms of such an approach are already well charted (an important analysis is Stephen Frosh, *Identity Crisis*, London: Macmillan, 1991). Perhaps the most obvious deficiency, especially as regards the theme of the self, is that such an approach pays scant regard to the emotional damage and psychic pain with which schizophrenia is routinely associated. The American critic James Glass, in his book *Shattered Selves* (1993), takes Deleuze and Guatarri to task for failing to recognize this tragic dimension of psychosis. For Glass, psychosis is not liberating or radically subversive; it is isolating and terrifying. To demonstrate these inner dreads, Glass paints a haunting portrait of a woman, Molly, suffering from psychosis and multiple personality disorder. In Molly's case, coldness, indifference and severe sexual abuse experienced at the hands of parental authority during her childhood were the precipitating factors to mental breakdown and eventual insanity. Her various alter egos or sub-personalities are examined by Glass as painful subjective reminders of such trauma, and he uses the case study to launch a powerful and compelling critique of Deleuze and Guatarri's postmodern slant on the schizo-multiple self.

Given the grievous psychological and political limitations of Deleuze and Guattari's celebration of schizophrenia, how should we characterize the general connections between postmodern culture and the self? An answer to this question, I have emphasized, must be careful to avoid a naive celebration of the multiplicity of selves, fragmented identities, narcissistic personality disorders and schizophrenia as possible subjective sources for alternative social arrangements. In espousing the need to free the self from any psychological, social or historical conceptions and idioms, this apparently 'radical' version of the postmodernist critique promotes a standpoint insensitive to the emotional costs of mental illness, as well as indifferent to the social harm of fragmentation. Seen in this way, the naturalistic philosophies of postmodern theorists such as Deleuze and Guatarri appear deterministic and bleak, and the social vision presented also seems politically vacuous.

Quite a different view of the postmodern self emerges, however, if we analyse contemporary culture in terms of the ambiguity, ambivalence, flux, dread and turmoil that shape the multilayered dynamics of modernity itself. What this conceptual move involves, in effect, is the recognition that the self is already a rich plurality of contending discourses, practices, images, fantasies and representations: a plurality constituted and reconstituted by contemporary social, cultural and political processes. It remains true, of course, that the notion of the self may be open to disruption from postmodernist and other current philosophical standpoints – that is to say, declarations about the 'death of the subject' or 'end of subjectivity' really do influence broader public perceptions and understandings of the self. It is not true, however, that the postmodernist playing with texts – of and by itself – reconfigures the complex relations between self, knowledge and power in the wider society. Rather than overestimate the social impact of the academy (something intellectuals are on occasion prone to do), this other brand of postmodernist thought concentrates upon transformations and crises discernible in the daily fabric of contemporary culture.

We can perhaps best illuminate the dominant understanding of postmodern culture, and its relation to the self, via the concept of what the French sociologist Jean Baudrillard (1929–2007) calls 'hyperreality'. The postmodern world for Baudrillard is a world of glittering media surfaces and radiant commodified images, a social environment in which all is transparent and explicit. The hyperreal he describes as a world of excess. It is a world where images become more powerful than reality, where everything is a copy of something else, and where the distinction between representation and what is represented is done away with. At the same time, core distinctions between self and object, inside and outside, surface and depth also vanish. For too long, social critics have treated the surface of social life as merely the superficial, as that which masks meaning. Baudrillard recommends that we abandon such a perspective, since, in the postmodern scenario, surfaces, images and simulations define the core of social experience. The hyperreality of media images is such that – thanks to virtual transformations concerning speed, quantity, size, etc. – traditional boundaries and classifications break down. Cultural objects take on new levels of fascination and the multiplication of media realities becomes overwhelming and extreme, so that reality-testing is in any event vacuous. Seduction lies at the core of Baudrillard's account of the hyperreal: fantasyscapes such as MTV, Disneyland and McDonald's become more vivid, more intense and more real than that which we typically think of as 'reality'.

In *Fatal Strategies* (1983), Baudrillard argues that images and simulations have become so intoxicating, so compelling and so seductive that the self is crushed. In referring to seduction, Baudrillard is careful to distinguish himself from Freud's use of the term. The postmodern process of seduction for Baudrillard refers not to the psychic economy of the self, but to the powers of fascination that objects hold over us. In our media-saturated economy, signs refer not to 'reality', but to themselves – and on and on, in an infinite regress. For example, the very idea of Coca-Cola – the 'Real thing' – holds more power and seductiveness than does the actual drink. Moreover, the world of things is constantly accelerating, changing form, structure, shape and boundaries. Fashion is taken to extreme by 'supermodels'; politics is redefined for a mass society in terrorism; sex is out-fantasized in pornography; and, the body undergoes transmutation in genetic cloning.

We should not be surprised to learn that the hyperreal extends to the very structure of human experience, locking perception into a new terrain of seduction, hallucination and virtualization. As the electronic mediation of TV screens and the Internet intensify, the self becomes a mere spectator, watching the endless images of mass culture with a mixture of delight and disdain. According to Baudrillard, the self that receives information is lifeless, bored, drained and atomized. In our decentralized world of communication, individuals cannot master – let alone control – the cultural logic governing information diffusion. The reason for this is clear enough for Baudrillard: the world is out of control, and all attempts to rationalize, conceptualize or theorize must fail. The most individuals can do is channel-hop, surf the Net, or mindlessly absorb the inanities of American-dominated pop culture. This situation Baudrillard sharply contrasts with the world of modernity. The modern sense of self was constructed around subjective elements, such as the passions, guilt and conscience, or the Freudian unconscious; against this backdrop meanings were attached to identity as concealed or hidden, with depth of self or interiority a key theme.

Unlike the modern sense of self, however, the postmodern self for Baudrillard celebrates appearance, exhibition, display and the aesthetics of style. Indeed, the seductive powers of style and image define the postmodern self through and through; there is no repressed self or depth of meaning, since in the new postmodern universe all is explicit, marked, seen and imaged.

Baudrillard's views have been sharply criticized on a number of grounds. Here I shall confine myself to a critical evaluation relevant to the theme of self-identity and the self. My critical comments can be divided into three categories.

First, Baudrillard's social theory is based upon an impoverished conception of the self. His claim that the self becomes more and more dissolved and dispersed as the world becomes increasingly globalized and mediated has important limitations, particularly for grasping the political consequences of postmodern media culture – as I will argue shortly. But it is especially deficient for understanding how the individual constructs a self out of symbolic materials and emotions experienced in active relation to the social world. Lost is the sense in which individuals explore alternative possibilities, fantasize new worlds for self-experimentation and autonomy and experiment with different definitions of the self. In Baudrillard's hypermediated world, the self is primarily a passive entity that thinks and feels in accordance with the 'code' of the dominant symbolic systems. Part of Baudrillard's inadequacy here, in my opinion, is that his account of the self is too strongly influenced by post-structuralist thought – and I say this despite the various criticisms of post-structuralism made by Baudrillard himself. By fixing the self in relation to the floating signifiers of simulation, Baudrillard views language and representation as refracted entirely through media culture. Yet such a standpoint shows little awareness of other forms of human activity and social practice. The self does not exist only 'in' media saturation; although the media are undoubtedly important in affecting transformations of self-identity. The self is anchored in, and experienced in relation to, the day-to-day contexts of routine social life. There is thus no logical reason why recognition of the multiple contexts of media and communication should be regarded as dissolving the symbolic continuity and emotional threads of the self.

Second, extending the previous argument, it is incorrect to assume, as Baudrillard seems to do, that media and cultural production today stands over and above individuals to such a degree that the philosophy of subjectivity is rendered obsolete. Baudrillard's argument concerning the supremacy of objects, media simulations and hyperreality is particularly evident in *Fatal Strategies*, but again there are deficiencies in such a view. It is surely the case that, thanks to the impact of globalization and new communication technologies, both self-identity and the basic organization of social relations begin to alter. Daily life is now suffused with communications. People watch videos, use computers, send faxes and attend to their email on the Internet. Electronic communications can be stored and retrieved in an instant, and such interconnection between people is today far less subject to constraints of time and space. There has been a considerable amount of recent sociological research, however, which highlights the view that media and cultural production cut two ways in relation to the self. On the one hand, the impact of mass popular culture, and the atomization connected with the fostering of niche lifestyle markets, can have a very draining, debilitating effect upon an individual's sense of self – as Baudrillard rightly emphasizes. On the other hand, postmodern forms of media and communication sometimes carry politically mobilizing consequences as regards the self. The assault on Rodney King by police in Los Angeles in 1991 is a case in point. The beating of King, a black man, by police was captured on home video by a person who happened to be nearby; the media subsequently screened the video. The importance of this event for the current discussion is that, not only did it propel events out of the control of local authorities, but it raised questions about the connections between identity, race and power the world over. The Rodney King affair was not simply passively absorbed by the masses; it was catapulted, because of public concern, into a matter of national and international importance. Yet it is precisely such socio-symbolic questioning and reconstruction of the self which Baudrillard's excessively pessimistic account – with its stress on apathy, boredom and inertia – fails to theorize.

Third, Baudrillard's exaggerated formulations concerning the fate of selfhood raise, in turn, further questions about the adequacy of his social analysis. The American critic Douglas Kellner has posed the interesting question of whether Baudrillard's work is best treated as science fiction or social theory. Whichever of these one opts for, it is most likely that Baudrillard will come to be seen as projecting his own inner desires and fantasies on those glittering objects of our media culture by which he is held enthralled. Seduced, indifferent, bored, stupefied: these are emotional states of the self, yet in the hands of Baudrillard they are described as the properties of cultural objects and events.

Strategies of the Self: Modern and Postmodern

It is now time to make a fuller assessment of the foregoing analysis of the self in postmodernity. In the work of Baudrillard, and many others who have developed analyses of postmodernity, the self becomes increasingly fluid, dispersed, multiple and fragmented. Yet have we, in fact, taken leave of the modern self? Have we entered, as some have argued, a social environment in which postmodern selfhood rules? I would answer 'no' to both questions. In a world of pervasive globalization and hi-tech media, the personal or subjective dimensions of social relations undergo extensive transformation – that much is surely clear. But this does not necessarily spell the end of modern identity; it may well indicate that the modern sense of self is becoming radicalized, or pushed to an extreme. The same might be said of the postmodernist thesis. Our cultural condition is not simply one of dislocation and fragmentation per se. On the contrary, we are living at a time in which we see the emergence of new strategies of the self, new ways of personal living and communal belonging.

The Polish sociologist Zygmunt Bauman (b. 1925) has argued that proclamations about the death of the self are sociologically naive. In a series of important books, including *Modernity and Ambivalence* (1991), *Postmodern Ethics* (1993) and *Life in Fragments* (1995), Bauman argues against a reading of postmodern identity as a cultural phase beyond modernist selfhood. He contends that contemporary culture – not without contradiction and tension – deploys both modern and postmodern strategies of identity. According to Bauman, the guiding impulse of the modern self is that of mastery. The desire for mastery takes the self into the controlled and controlling world of rationality and rational decision-making. The modern self is a self defined as a *project*: identity is framed carefully, systematically and painstakingly, with long-term planning and final objectives the key. In its order-building endeavours, the modern self is obsessed with stability, reliability, consistency and predictability. However, this search for self-mastery is, according to Bauman, self-defeating, illusory and fictitious. The desire for the ideal self (complete, finished, self-identical) leads women and men to believe that things can always be better, that identities can be more solid and ordered, that life can function more smoothly. This in turn leaves people feeling dissatisfied with the present, alienated from social relations and constrained in their self-expression.

By contrast, the postmodern self for Bauman is identity set adrift, lacking in solidity, continuity and structure. In our media-saturated world, different selves can now be adopted and discarded at whim, as the modern task of painstaking identity construction gives way to postmodern indifference, aloofness and scepticism. Bauman summarizes the postmodern self as the avoidance of fixed identity and ordered structure in the following way:

> To keep the game short means to beware long-term commitments. To refuse to be 'fixed' one way or the other. Not to get tied to one place, however pleasurable the present stop-over may feel. Not to wed one's life to one vocation only. Not to swear consistency and loyalty to anything or anybody. Not to control the future, but refuse to mortgage it: to take care that the consequences of the game do not outlive the game itself, and to renounce responsibility for such consequences as do. To forbid the past to bear on the present. In short, to cut the present off at both ends, to sever the present from history. To abolish time in any other form but of a loose assembly, or an arbitrary sequence, of present moments; to flatten the flow of time into a continuous present. . . . The hub of post-modern life strategy is not making identity stand – but the avoidance of being fixed. (Zygmunt Bauman, *Postmodernity and its Discontents*, Cambridge: Polity, 1997, p. 89)

Such deconstruction of the self leaves identities floating in a realm of fleeting moments, transitory encounters, eternal presents.

Bauman rejects the viewpoint that the postmodern spells a twilight for the self. That is to say, he rejects the radical postmodernist thesis concerning the wholly fragmented nature of postmodern culture. Instead, he sees postmodernity as bane and chance for the self. There is an intrinsic ambivalence at the heart of our cultural condition, he says, an ambivalence with which it is often excruciatingly painful to live. No wonder, then, that much of human history has been dedicated to designing ways of wiping out such pain – of which modernist identity strategies of mastery and control are signal examples. In the modern era this has meant legislating an ethical code for the self that would establish a world free from moral ambivalence. Such a code offered a direct escape from a lot of anxious groping in the dark over moral matters, precisely because modern ethical rules governing self-conduct provided practical help in achieving moral certitude. Not so postmodern forms of selfhood, however. After the demise of the modern, foundational ethical code governing the regulation of the self, life in postmodern times becomes increasingly fraught and ambivalent. There are no clear-cut answers anymore; people have to face moral ambivalence all over again, by design or by default.

This is not to suggest that postmodern forms of identity are easily achieved, however. As Bauman highlights, moral dilemmas of the self are continually shifted back to the marketplace in conditions of postmodernity. Expert promises of how to lead a life free from the strains of ambivalence are bought and sold, in matters concerning the ethics of the self as much as any other area of life. Bauman refers to this as the *privatization* of self. Against the backdrop of privatization, moral reasoning and evaluation become little more than responding to the task at hand, with technical forms of rationality dominant; we attempt to clear up the mess of yesterday's actions, but only in order to get on with tomorrow. And we act without giving ourselves enough time to think of the long-term effects of our doings – upon the self, other people or society at large. Such a privatization of the self would seem to suggest that we are all in unbelievable trouble, condemned to inhabit a social universe without subjective meaning, interpersonal commitment or ethical value. But Bauman cleverly insists that the political stakes of postmodernity involve, essentially, our collective attempts to go all the way through privatization, and to see (without any guarantees) whether we can emerge somewhere on the other side. His suggestion is that today we are left with questions, where once there appeared to be only answers – and that this is the postmodern enigma of identity or the self. Against the backdrop of globalization and new information technologies, we are collectively seeing the emergence of new kinds of moral question that the self has not previously had to face. What social good or ill, for instance, might artificial insemination and in vitro fertilization carry for future understandings of selfhood? How will new communication technologies affect intimacy, sexuality and the self? Bauman thinks that postmodern forms of self represent a chance, although a slim one, for a better world. While he recognizes that the ills of present-day society may be beyond the coping capacities of humanity, his analysis of modern and postmodern life strategies reveals that what finally comes to pass will involve the redefinition of self-identity and culture, and not simply of orthodox politics itself.

If ambivalence, ambiguity and uncertainty define contemporary states of mind, then the analysis of the internal instabilities and fissures of the self clearly moves to prominence as a core concern of the social sciences. Again, psychoanalysis has played an especially valuable role in contributing to a critical and comprehensive examination of the postmodern self. The dialogue established between psychoanalysis and postmodernist theory has turned out to be popular in many strands of social and cultural analysis, in part because of the very rich description of the psychological responses to social conditions that Freudianism offers. As discussed in chapter 2, Freud's theory of the self is built upon an intrinsic conflict between conscious rationality on the one hand and unconscious desire on the other. To understand self-experience is, in the Freudian frame, to investigate the clash between conscious and unconscious representation, emotion, desire, anxiety and defence – primarily as these are manifested in conceptions of the self, in interpersonal relationships and in dealings with the social environment. One central preoccupation in the dialogue between psychoanalysis and postmodernist theory has been the extent to which contemporary cultural conditions facilitate the questioning or enlarging of psychic space. To speak of the enlarging of psychic space, in this context, is to refer to the self-examination of experience in conjunction with the unconscious fantasies that colour how that experience is made sense of and reflected upon. Therapy is itself an excellent example of such a form of the probing of psychic space, or at least this is true in theory. By functioning as a kind of 'container' for distressing projections and destructive fantasies, the therapist can help the patient to think about – that is, to tolerate and manage – frightening emotional experience that previously needed to be excluded from psychic space by repression. Especially if both patient and therapist can remain open to such unwanted emotional transactions, then new forms of thinking and fresh conceptions of the self are likely to emerge from the therapeutic encounter.

Can we speak of postmodernism as providing such opportunities for the enlarging of psychic space? Some authors have suggested as much, seeing in the postmodern valorization of difference, heterogeneity, ambiguity and plurality a vibrant cultural condition that promotes the reflective self. The globalization of media, plurality of lifestyles, erosion of distinctions between high and low culture, and transformations in intimacy: we witness in this pluralistic world a radical questioning of the self, especially fantasies that influence anxieties and desires in relation to the social world. Other authors, however, have warned against an overly optimistic view of postmodernism. For these commentators, the convergence of psychoanalytic insight and analysis of postmodernism reveals a world devoid of meaning, of shattered experience, of inner turmoil. In this way of looking at the psychic costs of postmodernism, it is the failure of contemporary culture to provide people with adequate forms of emotional containment that is pivotal. Finding our way through present-day uncertainties has become so difficult, or so some commentators argue, that it is necessary to close down emotionally. (For critical assessments of this debate, see Anthony Elliott and Charles Spezzano (eds), *Psychoanalysis at its Limits: Navigating the Postmodern Turn*, London: Free Association Books, 2000.)

I think that authors who take either a solely optimistic or a pessimistic slant on postmodern identity can be criticized for closing themselves off from the complexity and contradiction of contemporary social processes. In my view, psychoanalysis is best used in conjunction with postmodernist theory to probe the complex, contradictory ways in which experience of the self is at once enlarged and threatened in the contemporary epoch. In a previous book, *Subject to Ourselves* (1996), I developed the argument that the advent of postmodernity is ambivalent in its emotional and political implications. The postmodern brings new opportunities for personal, aesthetic and moral life, but it also brings new risks and dangers. Drawing upon recent developments in psychoanalytic research, I suggested that this is especially evident in terms of tracking the fate of the self. For new technologies and postmodern aesthetics can extend the richness of the sense-making process, furthering the pre-existing categories by which we construct personal and cultural life. Postmodern selfhood, characterized by the chronic intrusion of self-reflexivity upon social life, is a state of mind receptive to other selves, without the psychic need for certitude and order, and with remarkable tolerance for ambivalence and ambiguity. There is considerable evidence that many contemporary cultural phenomena are premised upon, and further promote, such emotionally receptive selves. This is especially the case in the spheres of the visual and literary arts today, but it is also evident in matters relating to sexuality, gender, the family, friendship and cultural association more generally.

However, contemporary culture is not cut from one cloth. The rapidity of social change, and the uncertainties promoted by globalization and multiculturalism, can quickly overshadow the emotional capacities of individuals. Where individuals feel threatened or assaulted by social and technological upheavals, toleration of personal differences and cultural particularities sometimes diminishes. Excessive projection occurs, meaning is attacked, reflective thinking is refused. One of the ways in which the self can try to evade such anxiety is to avoid the difficulties of interpersonal relationships altogether, retreating to the comforting realm of narcissism in order to protect the self against fears of abandonment. The narcissistic self should thus be defined in opposition to postmodern identity. For the narcissistic self is an identity in which an individual's relation to others and the wider world is defined by attempting to control, order and master the flow of experience; such a self cannot easily tolerate ambivalence or complexity.

In some of my recent writings with the American sociologist Charles Lemert, notably *The New Individualism: The Emotional Costs of Globalization* (2005), we have sought to broaden the debate over the self in conditions of postmodernity by examining how individuals react to, and cope with, pressures arising from globalization. Our contention, broadly speaking, is that throughout the polished, expensive cities of the West there is an emergent 'new individualism' centred on continual self-actualization and instant self-reinvention. Today, this is nowhere more evident than in the pressure consumerism puts on us to 'transform' and 'improve' every aspect of ourselves: not just our homes and gardens, but our careers, our food, our clothes, our sex lives, our faces, minds and bodies. This reinvention trend occurs all around us, not only in the rise of plastic surgery and the instant identity makeovers of reality TV, but also in compulsive consumerism, speed dating and therapy culture. In a world that places a premium on instant gratification, the desire for immediate results has never been as pervasive or acute. We have become accustomed to corresponding by email across the planet in seconds, buying flashy consumer goods with the click of a mouse and drifting in and out of relations with others without long-term commitments. Is it any wonder that we now have different expectations about life's possibilities and the potential for change?

What are the broader social forces sustaining this new individualism? We suggest three key institutional features impinging on people's emotional experiences of globalization: consumerism, neo-liberalism and privatization. In conditions of advanced globalization, our language for expressing individualism is more and more fixed into the syntax of possession, ownership, control and market value. What we are suggesting is that people today increasingly suffer from an emotionally pathologizing version of neo-liberalism. What is pathological is the blinkered fixation on *instant change* – whether of the body, selfhood or society. The desire for instant reinvention of the self, Lemert and I argue, links to much broader institutional transformations of the world order. For the culture of globalization, as Richard Sennett rightly notes, is governed by the logic of acute short-termism.

Authors such as Sennett see the flexibility demanded of
workers by multinational corporations as demonstrating the
reality of globalization, promoting a dominant conception of
individuals as dispensable and disposable. But, we argue,
Sennett fails critically to probe just how far down the global
ethos of short-termism penetrates the emotional landscape of
the self. For it is precisely the emergence of an ambient fear
of disposability – of not measuring up to the craze for reinvention in personal and intimate life, family and work – that
fuels the emergence of 'the new individualism'. This is a form
of individualism based on a new cultural imperative for
people to be more efficient, faster, leaner, inventive and self-
actualizing than they were previously – not sporadically, but
day-in, day-out. Such an imperative lends to social life a radically experimental quality, with the thrills and spills of the
new individualism to the fore. But the emotional costs are
also high, and indeed many of the stories we recount of contemporary women and men in *The New Individualism* are
those of personal confusion, intense anxiety and disquieting
depression. Such emotional tribulations are not simply private
problems, however, as the new individualism is first and
foremost a consequence of our world of intensive globalization. In smashing apart traditional national boundaries,
globalization, ironically, offers people a kind of 'absolute
freedom' to do whatever they like. The irony is that the world
of 'everything goes' has become crippling, as the anxiety of
choice floats unhinged from both practical and ethical considerations as to what is worth pursuing. For those enticed
and seduced by the new individualism, the danger of self-
reinvention is a form of change so rapid and so complete that
identity becomes disposable. Instead of finding ourselves, we
lose ourselves.

  The notion of individuals struggling with a new individualism helps us to see, once again, that contemporary identity
strategies are never simply dichotomous: the new does not
simply transcend the traditional; the postmodern does not
simply eclipse the modern. Traditional and new individualisms, modern and postmodern forms of self, are better seen
as simultaneous ways of living in contemporary culture. Constructing a self today is about managing some blending of
these different ways of living; a kind of constant intermixing,

and dislocation, of modern and postmodern states of mind. If, for example, the term 'globalization' can today be used to fashion identities framed upon a sense of economic interconnectedness, democratic cosmopolitanism and a postnational way of belonging, it can also easily be deployed in a more defensive manner, the production of identities held in thrall to fundamentalism or the flag.

The relevance of modern and postmodern methods of negotiating the new individualism are great indeed. But in the social sciences it is crucial, I would argue, to keep a check on our ingrained urge to isolate and categorize the world according to pre-defined conceptual schemes. Again, Bauman develops this point well:

> What is in real life an agonizingly confused, contradictory and often incoherent state of affairs, may be portrayed as endowed with simple and regular features. . . . We do not live, after all, once in a pre-modern, once in a modern, once in a postmodern world. All three 'worlds' are but abstract idealizations of mutually incoherent aspects of the single life-process which we try our best to make as coherent as we can manage. Idealizations are no more (but no less either) than sediments, and also indispensable tools, of those efforts. (Z. Bauman, *Mortality, Immortality and Other Life Strategies*, Cambridge: Polity, 1992, p. 11)

It will not do, in other words, to define the self as either modern, late modern or postmodern. For one can see a formidable mixture of such identities at work everywhere. Modern states of mind and forms of self continue, often in the grip of an insanely self-destructive, violent rationality – as ethnic and nationalist conflicts across the globe powerfully underline. But so too do we glimpse post-traditional, postmodern ways of living together, as well as the spread of new individualisms in corporate networking and compulsive consumerism.

It is true that we may not yet be living in a fully postmodern era, but glimpses of a postmodern social universe are available for all to see. The challenge now for social scientists is to confront the pluralism and diversity of the postmodern self, or selves, anew, in a context of altered social circumstances sweeping the globe.

Conclusion

In the preceding chapters I have sought to introduce the reader to various concepts of the self. In terms of social critique, the discourses I have examined – from sociological approaches to postmodernism, from psychoanalysis to queer theory – profoundly challenge the assumptions of mainstream social science; these discourses, in very different ways, cross disciplinary boundaries and promote new cultural criticism concerned with identity, imagination, intimacy, gender and sexual difference. The question remains, however, as to how to account for the mediation of self and society, as well as the reshaping of self in the age of identity politics. Drawing together some of the arguments sketched earlier, I shall conclude by considering fresh opportunities for, and current limitations on, theorizing identity categories and the self.

Inner Depth, or Inside Out

There are some writers who argue that psychoanalysis has contributed more to the development of a critical theory of the self than any other theoretical paradigm in the social sciences. This is not a view I share, for reasons I have discussed in detail elsewhere (see my *Social Theory and Psychoanalysis in Transition*, London: Free Association Books, 1999).

Notwithstanding the essential importance of Freud's writings on the self to social theory, together with the social sciences in general, there are fundamental problems and incoherencies in Freudian thought which can be adequately resolved, I believe, only by drawing on the current diversity of critical social theories. The tension in Freud's thought between the split and fractured nature of unconscious desire, on the one hand, and the transhistorical symbolic anchorage of sexual difference and moral norms, on the other, is a good example of this. For the radical psychological and cultural insights contained in many of Freud's writings, fuelled by his conceptual underlining of the fractured and unstable terrain of individual subjectivity, are (at times) cancelled out by his more culturally conservative theorizing, in respect of both the power of internalized moral norms and the immutable force of sexual difference. While Freud occasionally refers to social institutions and political life, the main tendency of his work is to analyse the contradiction between desire and culture as solely emanating from the unconscious, the superego, or the psyche. We only occasionally catch a flavour with Freud of the complex ways in which identity and the self are implicated in inscriptions of culture, and the forms through which culture and politics assign desires and dreads to people's lives. Since Freud, it has fallen to social theorists, cultural analysts, philosophers and feminists to take up the challenge that psychoanalytic theory poses for developing a conception of the self as split and conflicting, though many of the psychoanalytically informed cultural theories of self we have examined undoubtedly retain some of the more conservative tendencies of Freudian theory.

The sociological approaches I discussed in chapter 1 go some considerable distance towards challenging the idea that self-experience can be understood solely in terms of psychological dispositions or inner depth, because of the *shared symbolic meanings* that define day-to-day social life. In the work of Mead and other symbolic interactionists, the central dilemma of personal identity is that of balancing the multiple demands of society and culture on the self with inner definitions of identity; in Mead's terms, the 'I', or ego, seeks to limit the 'me', or social self, from cultural dislocation. In the work of Goffman, the dialogue between self and others is analysed as part of the theatre of social life, with identity conceptualized as a performance successfully accomplished. In the work of Giddens, self and reflexivity are intimately interwoven, such that social practices are continually examined and monitored in the course of daily life. These sociological ways of seeing the self put considerable emphasis on the tacit knowledge or local understandings of individuals engaged in social interaction. This is more than just an emphasis on the social construction of the self; the point, rather, is that identity is inherently and inescapably bound up with the practices, knowledge and information which defines it.

Offsetting such sociological critique, Foucault's work on sexuality and the self draws attention to the more socially manipulative, degraded and harmful aspects of self-constitution. Social practices are equated by Foucault with self-subjection – the various technologies of individual domination. Psychoanalysis, as we saw in the discussion of Foucault's work in chapter 3, offers itself as one such objectifying confessional technology, in which the 'truth' of the self is derived from scrutinizing desires, dreams and fictions in the sexual life of the individual. Taking seriously the dynamic character of how an individual acts upon himself or herself, Judith Butler similarly explores contortions of subjectivity by situating Foucault's work in relation to the performing self. Identifying Foucault's analyses of technologies of domination and power as reductive or rigid as regards the self, Butler turns to psychoanalytic theory to emphasize the role of fantasy at the centre of discourse, the body, situated doings, representations of gender, and performed identities.

It is interesting that Butler, like Foucault, does not attempt to transcend the binary oppositions – inside/outside, surface/depth, individual/society – that figure prominently in discourses of the self. Rather, she seeks to play such oppositions off against each other in order to formulate a radical account of performative identity: she traces, in effect, the self's illusions of 'inner depth' as generated by technologies of an outside, of discourse. Yet Butler's approach, while more sophisticated than orthodox Foucaultianism (primarily due to her interpretation of psychoanalytic narratives of self), lacks a treatment of both imagination and interpersonal relations as the source of radically novel psychic creations of the self. Her main preoccupation is rather with transgression, as a dispersion of the self. Like Foucault's, Butler's account of the self is one that is isolated and solitary. Self-constitution, self-stylization and self-performance occur in the work of Foucault and Butler as the self creating a relation with itself; the self is not conceptualized as inscribed in forms of creative social interaction.

A radical critical theory must, in my view, attempt to attain a more adequate understanding of the fissures and contradictions that permeate the psychic production of the self as this relates to the workings of identity in the social world. Now Butler's revised Foucaultianism is undeniably important in this respect; but it is not sufficient. It is not sufficient because the self cannot be reduced to performance. We can say with Butler, and also Goffman to be sure, that the self is fashioned through performance; and yet there are desires, affects and fantasies that disrupt the boundaries and borders of routine social interaction. Recognizing the power of the repressed unconscious requires a notion of self that is attentive to split-off or disowned aspects of identity (the internal other), as well as the myriad forms in which such frightening internal objects attach to external, social others. This blending of repudiated internal objects and external, denigrated others is precisely what accounts for the emotional force and political dynamism of ideologies of racism, sexism, nationalism and the like. To deconstruct identity in this manner is not to return to a romantic concept of self; nor does it involve accepting consumer rhetoric concerning 'the true self' or 'inner selves'. It involves, rather, an examination of the mobility and the fragility of identifications through which the self establishes a relation to identity, to others and to the social world. The sheer emotional and political complexity of this blend of internal identifications and external exclusions demands the rethinking of the conceptual frames used to analyse self or subjectivity.

The Foucaultian and postmodern critique of identity should not prevent critical analysis of the identifications and ideals that comprise psychic subjectivity. We need to connect some kind of radical Foucaultian narrative to psychoanalytic theory in order to supply a critical perspective on the self.

What we have to grasp is how social constructions of self are also imaginings of the psyche. In breaking with orthodox views which keep apart the social and the psyche, we have to grasp how social and cultural forms are given shape internally, which necessarily entails reflecting on how the self is constituted culturally as an expression of 'inner depth'. We need to see that unconscious imaginings of the self are always elaborated and framed within discourses and institutions. Selfhood is not determined or pre-packaged; rather, the self is a work of active construction and reconstruction, built on inner workings of fantasy and its unconscious contortions – anxieties about difference, about otherness and strangeness, about intimacy and proximity – in the wider frame of culture, society and politics. Saying this, however, immediately raises issues concerning the political implications of the critique of self and the future of identity politics.

Identity Politics, or Critique of Self

In his book *Liquid Modernity* (2000) Zygmunt Bauman contrasts the solidity and continuity which used to be the trademark of modern identities with the floating and drifting selves of postmodernism. In present-day postmodern society, argues Bauman, the dominant structure of feeling is that of uncertainty – uncertainties concerning the condition of the self, the moral geography of interpersonal relationships and the future shape of the world. According to Bauman, identity, including identity politics and its expression in new social movements, is today experienced as problematic (as open-ended, uncontrollable and hence with an overwhelming feeling of uncertainty) precisely because of the breakdown of modernist culture and its political attempts to legislate the world as cohesive, continuous and consistent. Identity politics develops as a preoccupation in the aftermath of the collapse of Western nation-state cultures; current claims for, and the advancement of, racial, ethnic, religious, national, postcolonial or sexual identities are an attempt to probe the many repressed differences of selfhood, differences brutally denied and displaced by the imposition of modernist Western culture on global political space.

The critical social theories I have examined in this book have an enormous amount to contribute to the study of identity politics, as well as the undoing of self-repudiations, of rewriting the relation between self and society, and of coming to social and political terms with the hopes and fears of present-day subjectivity and identity. The changing cultural parameters of identity politics, with its stress on the articulation of selfhood through processes of social and political location, highlight clearly why the self cannot be made sense of in strictly psychological or sociological terms, or some blending of the two. What is obvious from current cultural struggles over the fate of the self is the contested, tensional, critical and, above all, political nature of the process of identity-building. Twenty-first-century society is a world (to paraphrase Bauman) of light mobilities and liquid experiences, a world in which people, organizations, institutions, employment, entertainment, images, messages, money and the like are framed and positioned within global flows that undermine national, societal borders. This growing fluidity and liquidization of the social network carries serious implications for experiences of self, identity, interpersonal relationships and intimacy; the fluid state of identity politics is both an outcome and a potential alternative to this state of affairs, and raises new chances and risks for individual autonomy and collective social objectives.

Put this way, identity politics may well be more radical in its implications for self-autonomy than orthodox or institutional politics. Such a claim is, of course, highly contested in current intellectual and public debate; there is certainly no shortage of voices, on both the political left and right, that dismiss identity politics for its narcissistic preoccupation with self and personal experience, or for wandering too far from the big issues of capitalism, patriarchy or globalization. Yet the present-day crisis of the self is, I believe, at root a crisis in cultural practices and the right formally to occupy particular social spaces. Indeed, one of the achievements of identity politics – from the new feminism to queer theory to postmodern aesthetics – has been to foreground the importance of what once were highly subjective aspects of self-organization (such as imagination, desire or creativity) and link them to politics and culture in the broadest sense. Identity politics, far from being a narcissistic diversion in which the self closes in on itself, is a chance for self-interrogation, a chance for the probing of tacit cultural and political assumptions, and a chance for alternative futures.

But there are other difficulties that plague identity politics, or at least this is so when the concern of cultural politics with the self is viewed from the angle of orthodox, institutional politics. It is hard for many to fathom how cultures and conflicts of identity whose priorities are short term, provisional, ambivalent and even contradictory might produce emancipatory outcomes in order to promote the authentic affirmation of identities. Identity politics is thus said to live with a central paradox: that of wishing to assert or claim a distinctive identity, in the sense of taking individual selfhood and collective identity seriously, while also wanting to dismantle and critique the very notions of self, agency and identity. This is especially relevant at the present time, where debates over, say, postcolonialist identities or post-feminist selves routinely involve such doubleness – that is, going back over a past historical tradition and adopting certain themes and elements, while dismantling that very tradition in the act of looking ahead to something new. At a trivial level, this has led to the culture and consumption of New Identities, in which the free flight of fantasy appears in everything from self-help manuals to TV chat-shows. Identity tends to be associated in this context with a thirst for reinvention, reconstruction, restaging and reshaping. At a more interesting level, the doubleness of identity politics has spawned a variety of debates relating to modernist strategies of intensive self-construction (ordered, regular, predictable), and postmodern life strategies involving diversity, difference and discontinuity in interpersonal relationships and cultural pursuits.

From the current debate in the social sciences concerning the self, the link to identity politics is, as we have seen, by no means necessarily a progressive one and is certainly not guaranteed success. Many lament the transformation of the public sphere through current media-generated spectacles of private dramas and personal troubles; such a restructuring of the private and the public, so it is argued, results not in a *politicization of identity* but in a *privatization of politics*. The public sphere in this view is no longer a realm for resolving political conflict; instead, it is part of the commodification and privatization of identity problems, where such problems (despite gaining public attention for a fleeting moment) remain in check as *private issues*. For others, we are witnessing not the demise, but a rebirth of politics. Far from being an individualized realm of narcissistic self-absorption, the problematization of selves and identities has led to political structures being challenged by minority groups, by feminists, by gay and queer activists, by black studies, and by psychoanalytic and postmodern interventions. Selfhood, as we have seen, has passed over from being on the side of social order and social structure to the side of cultural difference, and is thus presented and experienced as a political problem. Seen from this angle, nothing could be further from the truth than the charge that self and identity are removed from the concerns of daily political life.

Afterword: Globalization, Postmodernization and New Individualism

This book was initially conceived and written in 2000, when the postmodern 1990s were drawing to a close but before various tumultuous world events were to unfold in the early days of the twenty-first century. The global impacts and fallout from 9/11, the wars in Afghanistan and Iraq, as well as deepening anxieties over climate change and fresh dangers of ecological and nuclear catastrophe, have all created a conjuncture of social despair, political pessimism and general impatience with the existing world. The influence of such social and political forces upon the fabric of lived experience has been profound, and consequently the messy realities of the self that I have charted throughout this book have become, arguably, messier. These developments are not just personal problems for people to attempt to resolve at the level of the self; they should be seen, politically, as at the core of any future programme for social change and also fundamental to the landscape of the self as well as the current 'new individualism' sweeping the globe.

These intersections between current political and personal changes spreading across modern societies carry important consequences for future trajectories of the self. Three such major trajectories are evident in our own time. First, territories of the self – both positive and negative – are being powerfully reshaped by our world of intensive globalization, and indeed it is my view that processes affecting the *globalization of self* are likely to intensify. This is not to say that what we see unfolding today is a uniformity of lived experience of the self. On the contrary, the task of a reflective social theory of the self, broadly speaking, is to take apart the received wisdom that globalization creates a flattening or diminution of lived experience and to probe the complex, contradictory global forces that shape our current ways of life and trajectories of self. In this sense, recent social theory has had much of interest to contribute to debates on selfhood, since various social analysts have detected signs that contemporary identities are moving in a more cosmopolitan, post-traditional or global direction. Such grand claims issuing from the realms of 'high theory' obviously need to be instantly qualified for a whole host of reasons. One would be that older generations do not necessarily fall within such a description of the world, if only for the reason that older generations in the West tend to be much more focused on the nation-state than younger people appear to be. By contrast, those who have been brought up with Yahoo, MTV and Starbucks are, and not surprisingly, more likely to affirm various identifications with global civil society. Yet it is far from clear that the consumption of globalization as currently promoted throughout the West can lead to sustaining, nourishing and, indeed, meaningful forms of self-identity. That is to say, the commercial and corporate aspects of globalized culture might be said to deprive people of a sense of meaningful identity. Yahoo, MTV and Starbucks may promote consumerist identities of various global kinds, but do not (as yet, at any rate) give rise to a fully fledged sense of self. This may of course change, and the globalization of identity may become deeply anchored in personal experience, with long-term consequences. At the current historical juncture, however, all of this is merely suggestive. The most that can be said, with any degree of confidence, is that concepts of self increasingly turn on a globalized pivot.

The second area where cultural and political forces have become closely interwoven with the fabric of the self is in the increased fragmentation or liquidity of personal and social experience. This refers, in the broadest sense, to a *postmodernization of self*. Of key importance in this respect are new information technologies, including amongst others the processes of digitization, the development of interactive media and satellite communication technology. Here the 'speeding up of the world', as represented in our media-saturated televisual environments, enters into the fabric of personal and emotional experience in complex ways. As we have seen, some social analysts view our hi-tech media cultures as mobilizing narcissistic elements of the self; other analysts view these trends as promoting closure of the self from civic and political participation. In the aftermath of 9/11 and the globalization of terrorism, there are strong indications of an erosion of the stable or taken-for-granted foundations governing daily life – one consequence of which has been more fragmentation in contemporary society, a fragmented self, a 'liquid life' in the apt phrase of Zygmunt Bauman. In this regard, the discourse of the self is not a matter of Baudrillard's hyperreality and the culture of denial, but a politics of experience, a rediscovery of the meaning-making capacities of the human mind coupled with a profound questioning of what is in people's minds and of the role of the mass media in shaping contemporary aspects of the self. Whether the self can cope with, and respond to, the increasing 'information overload' of a 24/7 media culture is a key political issue of our times.

The third and final area is that of emotional life and its relation to the self. An area long neglected by sociologists, the relation between emotion or affect and self has moved high on the agenda of much current social and cultural theory, and with good political reasons. The combined social transformations of globalization and postmodernism, as Charles Lemert and I argue at length in *The New Individualism*, has been transferred to thinking about the self primarily in terms of ever-increasing dynamism, speed, change and reinvention. From compulsive consumerism to therapy culture, from corporate life to cosmetic surgery, the concept of a sustained sense of self has been largely dismantled and replaced by the mantra of 'instant self-reinvention'. Here there is a direct line between the fragmenting world of globalization and the fragmented state of people's lives: the 'want-now' consumerism promoted by global corporate culture is held in thrall to a notion of immediacy which lies at the core of today's reinvention craze. And it is this reinvention craze, from self-help to psychotherapy, that is viewed by many as the way of the future for thinking about the shape of our lives and possibilities for the self. My quarrel with advocates of the new individualism is not whether these changes at the level of self are happening; clearly, these social changes are well under way and increasingly so across the polished, expensive cities of the West. My argument is that such changes are not necessarily positive; they also carry debilitating consequences for self-identity and the search for freedom. Indeed, exploration of the emotional consequences of the new individualism remains a core political challenge in our own time of globalization and widespread social uncertainty.

Index

action
  interpretations of 35
  rationality 15
Adler, Alfred
  original meaning of lifestyle
    12
aesthetics 110
  Foucault's self-construction
    100–1
agency
  experimenting with identity
    7
AIDS/HIV
  bodily self-management
    104–5
alienation
  of consumerism 78–80
Allen, Woody
  Zelig 41–2
Americanization 19, 22
*Anti-Oedipus: Capitalism and
  Schizophrenia* (Deleuze
  and Guattari) 147
anti-Semitism
  Žižek's analysis 83
The Archaeology of Knowledge
  (Foucault) 88

Aristotle 57
The Assault on Truth (Masson)
  70–1
Baudrillard, Jean
  critique of 151–3
  Fatal Strategies 149–50, 152
  hyperreality 149–51
Bauman, Zygmunt
  idealizations of the world
    161
  Life in Fragments 153
  Liquid Modernity 166
  Modernity and Ambivalence
    153
  Postmodern Ethics 153
  the postmodern project of
    identity 153–6
  privatization of self 155–6
Beauvoir, Simone de 18, 72
  and Butler 153–6
  The Second Sex 113–14
Benhabib, Seyla
  Situating the Self 14
Benkert, Karoly Maria 131
Bentham, Jeremy
  the panopticon 89

Birth of the Clinic (Foucault)
    88
Blumer, Herbert 29, 38
    'Society as Symbolic
        Interaction' 34–5
    symbolic interactionism
        34–7
the body
    political configuration 106
    self-regulation in postmodern
        culture 104–6
The Body and Society (Turner)
    104
Butler, Judith 17, 18, 21, 26
    Gender Trouble 124–30
    performative identity 164–5

capitalism, late
    consumerism and narcissism
        77–80
    dislocation 139–40, 144
    postmodernism 140–1, 143
    self in consumption 8
    Sennett on effects of
        globalization 138–41
    signs, codes and messages 24
    see also consumption
The Care of the Self (Foucault)
    96
Cascardi, Anthony
    The Subject of Modernity 14
Castoriadis, Cornelius
    *The Imaginary Institution of
        Society* 81–2
    *Philosophy, Politics,
        Autonomy* 82
Character Analysis (Reich) 75
childhood
    Chodorow on mothering
        113–20
    founding of 'lifestyle' 12
    Freudian sexual development
        59
    Kristeva on fantasies of
        maternity 120–4

Lacan's mirror-stage 60–2
Oepidal complex 62–7
psychosexual development
    100
symbolically defined roles 33
Winnicott's transitional
    relations 67–9
Chodorow, Nancy 18, 26
    creating self and gender
        115–20
    criticism of 118–20
    *Femininities, Masculinities,
        Sexualities* 64
    and Kristeva 123–4
    *The Reproduction of
        Mothering* 115–6
Civilization and its Discontents
    (Freud) 36, 73–4, 77
class 20
    site of subjectivity 23
Clough, Patricia 136
cognition
    basis of symbolic
        interactionism 35–6
Collins, Randall 43
Coming Out (Weeks) 131–2
communications technology 1,
    2, 22, 26
Baudrillard 152
    postmodernism 143, 144
    surveillance and management
        of identity 106–7
    Turkle on the internet
        141–2
*The Consequences of
    Modernity* (Giddens) 45
constructionism *see* Foucault,
    Michel
consumption 19, 22
    communications technology
        26
    defining self 2, 4, 8
    mass market lifestyles 12
    narcissism and detachment
        of 77–80

self-regulation of the body
104–6
conversation
learning attitudes of others
32
Cooley, Charles H. 30
The Corrosion of Character
(Sennett) 139–40
culture
assumptions about identity 8
deconstruction of self
17–18
fin de siècle European
repression 57
Freud conception of
development 73–5
global 143
moral conventions 64–5
postmodernism 158
reading the signs of 45
Reich and Marcuse 75–7
site of subjectivity 23
sixties and seventies politics
17–18
style 20
The Culture of Narcissism
(Lasch) 78

Deleuze, Gilles
*Anti-Oedipus: Capitalism
and Schizophrenia* (with
Guattari) 147
critique by Glass 148
denial 25
Dewey, John 30
'A Difficulty in the Path of
Psychoanalysis' (Freud)
56, 60
Discipline and Punish
(Foucault) 88, 89
discourse theory 19
displacement 25

ecology movements 19, 21
economics 2, 11

Elliott, Anthony
Freud 2000 69
*The New Individualism: The
Emotional Costs of
Globalization* (with
Lemert) 159–60,
171–2
*Psychoanalysis at its Limits:
Navigating the
Postmodern Turn* (with
Spezzano) 157
*Social Theory and
Psychoanalysis in
Transition* 162
Subject to Ourselves 158
emotions
affective ways of dealing
with others 52
dislocation 54–5
postmodern capacities
157–9
psychoanalytic theory
6–7
symbolic interactionism 35
Winnicot's transitional
relations 67–9
see also repression
Enlightenment rationality
110
The Epistemology of the Closet
(Sedgwick) 134–5
Eros and Civilization
(Marcuse) 76–7

families
reflexivity of Giddens
45–8
Winnicott on mothering
67–9
see also childhood; marriage
fantasy 166
Baudrillard's hyperreality
149–51
Freudian 70–1
postmodernism 145

fascism
  Reich's psychoanalytic
    analysis 75–6
  Fatal Strategies (Baudrillard)
    149–50, 152
  *Femininities, Masculinities,
    Sexualities* (Chodorow) 64
feminism 26
  Butler's peformative theory
    124–30
  conflicts between women 21
  creation of self and gender
    115–20
  criticism of Freudian
    psychoanalysis 71–2
  formation of identity 130–1
  Foucault perspective 101–2
  identity politics 20–1
  link to political culture
    167–9
  and psychoanalysis 26,
    112–15
  self-formation 13, 16–7
Fichte, Johann Gottlieb 57
Flax, Jane
  Thinking Fragments 72
food
  diet and discipline 104–6
  eating disorders 106
Foucault, Michel
  aesthetic self-construction
    100–1
  *The Archaeology of
    Knowledge* 88
  Birth of the Clinic 88
  The Care of the Self 96
  classical world and sexuality
    96–7
  construction of self 36–7,
    100–1, 164–5
  debunks 'repressive
    hypothesis' 92–6
  Discipline and Punish 88,
    89

Freudian social control 71
  'governmentality' 103–4
  The History of Sexuality
    91–4, 103
  homosexuality 97–8
  influence on others 104,
    106, 124, 126, 128
  Madness and Civilization 88
  The Order of Things 88
  power relations and
    discipline 26, 89–91
  sexuality and social control
    99–103, 109
  technologies of the self
    110–11
  The Use of Pleasure 96
fragmentation
  Deleuze and Guattari on
    schizophrenia 147
  feature of postmodernism
    145
  Lacan's splintered mirror
    145–7
Freud, Sigmund 17, 19, 21
  attitudes towards 55
  charge of conservativism 71
  *Civilization and its
    Discontents* 36, 73–4,
    77
  conscious *versus* unconscious
    156–7
  conventions and culture
    64–5
  cultural development 73–5
  'A Difficulty in the Path of
    Psychoanalysis' 56, 60
  discovers the hidden self
    56–7
  emotional inconsistency 55
  life and death drives 74
  little account of external,
    social conditions 69–70
  masculinity and femininity
    114–15

Oedipus complex 62–7, 79, 119, 112
'An Outline of Psycho-Analysis' 60
scientific status of psychoanalysis 58–60
self and social theory 163
self-love 80
sexual contradiction 55
social order *versus* personal happiness 86
Totem and Taboo 73
unconscious desires 10, 35–6, 73
see also psychoanalytic theory
Freud 2000 (Elliott) 69
Friedan, Betty 72
Frosh, Stephen
Identity Crisis 147–8
Fuss, Diana 133–4, 135

gay men *see* homosexuality; queer theory
gender 26
Chodorow on mothering 113–20
Foucault on 101–2
Freudian development 63–7
Kristeva on mothering 120–4
power relations and sex 97
reproduction 112–13
site of subjectivity 23
see also feminism
Gender Trouble (Butler) 124–30
Giddens, Anthony 25, 31
background 44–5
The Consequences of Modernity 45
criticism of 48–50
double hermeneutic 11

Modernity and Self-Identity 44, 48, 80
reflexivity of self 44–50, 51–2, 80, 164
The Transformation of Intimacy 44
Glass, James
Shattered Selves 148
globalism 19
identity politics 21–2, 166
postmodernism 160–1
Sennett's late capitalism 138–41
globalization 2, 3, 19, 21–2, 52, 158–61, 169–72
Goethe, Johann Wolfgang von 57
Goffman, Erving 17, 25, 40ff.
Asylums 41–2
and Butler 128
critiques of 43–4
dialogue between self and others 163–4
manipulation of appearances 51
performance 165
The Presentation of Self in Everyday Life 38–9
production of self and roles 37–44
response cries 40
'role distance' and 'faces' 39–40
and symbolic interactionism 38
'total institution' 41
Gouldner, Alvin
critique of Goffman 42
Governing the Soul (Rose) 107–8
'The Government of the Body' (Turner) 105–6
Greece, classical
sexuality 96–7

Greer, Germaine 72
Guattari, Felix
    *Anti-Oedipus: Capitalism
        and Schizophrenia* (with
        Deleuze) 147
    critique by Glass 148

happiness *versus* social order
    86
hermeneutics, double 11
The History of Sexuality
    (Foucault) 91–4, 103
homosexuality 16, 20
    Butler's performative gender
        126, 127–8
    classical Greece 97
    formation of sexual identity
        130–3
    Foucault 97–8
    Kristeva on maternal
        fantasies 122–3
    language denoting identity
        131
    Oepidal complex 62–3
    politics of 132–7
human rights movements 20
hyperreality
    Baudrillard 149–53

identity
    Bauman's postmodern
        project 153–6
    Butler discards from
        feminism 124–6
    collective 14
    cultivation of sexual
        behaviour 95
    culture of homosexuality 98
    experimenting with 7
    fluid 9
    fragmentation and
        dislocation 138–41
    internet interchangeability
        141–2

    meanings 13–14
    symbolic project 19
    see also sexuality
Identity Crisis (Frosh)
    147–8
identity politics 165–6
    collapse of nation-state
        cultures 166
    many aspects of 20–1
    postmodernism 143
    privatized 23, 167–9
    see also feminism; race and
        ethnicity
ideology
    construction of identity 19
*The Imaginary Institution
    of Society* (Castoriadis)
    81–2
imagination and creativity
    Castoriadis on 81–2
    Winnicott on 68
individuals
    alienation of consumerism
        78–80
    Giddens and 48
    and psychotherapy 85–6
    'information overload' 3,
        171
information technology *see*
    communications
    technology
institution
    prisons and surveillance
        89–91
    social control 88–9
interaction
    daily life 28–9
    Mead's symbolic 31–4
Inventing Our Selves (Rose)
    107–8

Jacoby, Russell
    Social Amnesia 71
James, William 30

Kellner, Douglas 152
Kertbeny, Karl 131
King, Rodney 152
knowledge
  rationality 15
Kohut, Heinz 80
Kovel, Joel 79
Kristeva, Julia 18, 21, 26
  and Chodorow 123–4
  motherhood and gender
    identity 120–4
  'Stabat Mater' 121–2

Lacan, Jacques
  and Butler 124
  influence on Žižek 82
  language and gender identity
    119
  mirror stage 60–2,
    145–6
  'The Mirror-stage as
    Formative of the Function
    of the I' 60–2
  re-fashions Oedipal complex
    65–6
  social interactionism 37
  splintered postmodern
    selfhood 145–7
language
  denoting sexual identity 119,
    131
  of homosexuality 134–5
  poetry 32
  structuralism 25–6
  see also symbolic
    interactionism
Lasch, Christopher 15
  consumer capitalism and
    narcissism 78–80
  The Culture of Narcissism
    78
  The Minimal Self 78
leisure
  defining self 8

Lemert, Charles
  *The New Individualism: The
    Emotional Costs of
    Globalization* (with Elliott)
    159–60, 171–2
  *Postmodernism is not what
    You Think* 22
lesbians *see* homosexuality;
  queer theory
liberationist politics 19
Life in Fragments (Bauman)
  153
Life on the Screen (Turkle)
  141–2
lifestyle
  changing meanings 12
Liquid Modernity (Bauman)
  166

McNay, Lois
  Foucault's aesthetic self-
    construction 100–1
Madness and Civilization
  (Foucault) 88
Marcuse, Herbert 17, 21, 29,
  75
  culture, sexuality and
    repression 76–7
  Eros and Civilization 76–7
  surplus-repression 86
marriage
  constructive renewal of
    divorce 47–8
  reflexivity of Giddens
    45–8
  see also families
Marx, Karl
  all that is solid 143–4
mass media 2–3, 22
  Baudrillard on hyperreality
    149–53
  postmodernism 145
*The Mass Psychology of
  Fascism* (Reich) 75

Masson, Jeffrey
  The Assault on Truth 70–1
Mead, George Herbert 29
  context and influences
    30–1
  'I' and 'me' 33–4
  Mind, Self and Society 31
  symbolic interactionism 24,
    31–4, 50, 163
  weakness of theory 35–7
migration 19, 22
Mind, Self and Society (Mead)
  31
The Minimal Self (Lasch) 78
'The Mirror-stage as Formative
  of the Function of the I'
  (Lacan) 60–2
Mitchell, Juliet
  Psychoanalysis and Feminism
  72
Modernity and Ambivalence
  (Bauman) 153
Modernity and Self-Identity
  (Giddens) 44, 48, 80
morality
  contemporary marriage and
    family 46–8
  conventions and culture
    64–5
  Goffman's performative self
    42
  late capitalism 139
  modern self-mastery 155
  new questions 156
Morris, Meghan 101–2
multiculturalism 19, 20

narcissism
  Lacan's mirror-stage 60–2
  Lasch on consumer
    capitalism and 78–80
  postmodern 158–9
'new individualism' 159–61,
  171–2

*The New Individualism:
  The Emotional Costs of
  Globalization* (Elliott and
  Lemert) 159–60, 171–2
'The New You' competition
  7–8
Nietzsche, Friedrich
  on the hidden self 56

Oedipus complex 62–7, 79
  feminism and gender identity
    119, 121
The Order of Things
  (Foucault) 88
other people's viewpoints 32
'An Outline of Psychoanalysis'
  (Freud) 60

panopticon
  Bentham's 89
  Poster's communication
    technology 106–7
peace movements 21
Peirce, Charles S. 30
performance
  Butler's performative identity
    164–5
  Goffman's dramatic roles
    37–44
philosophy 15
Philosophy, Politics, Autonomy
  (Castoriadis) 82
physical self
  bodily management 40
poetry 32
politics
  anti–political 23
  deconstruction of self
    17–18
  fabrication of the subjective
    14
  of homosexuality 132–7
  liberationist 19
  reconfigured as personal 18

Reich's psychoanalytic
    analysis 75–6
Žižek's formation of identity
    82–4
see also identity politics
post-structuralism
    Baudrillard 151
    decentring the subject 19
    external formation of self 10
    Giddens's individualism 48
Poster, Mark 110
    surveillance and
        communication technology
        106–7
Postmodern Ethics (Bauman)
    153
postmodernism 27
    Baudrillard's hyperreality
        149–53
    Bauman's project of identity
        153–6
    emotional capacities
        157–9
    fantasy and phantasmagoria
        145
    features of 143–5
    Giddens's individualism 48
    internet identities 141–2
    late capitalist fragmentation
        140–1, 145
    link to political culture 156
    mass media 145
    multiplications of narratives
        7
    personal identity 19–20
    and psychoanalytic theory
        156–7
    psychology and culture 13
    schizophrenia 147–8
*Postmodernism is not what
    You Think* (Lemert) 22
power relations
    Foucault on 25–6, 89–91
    men and women 96

and sexual behaviour 92–3
site of subjectivity 23
*The Presentation of Self in
    Everyday Life* (Goffman)
    38–9
Priscilla: Queen of the Desert
    (film) 129
prisons
    Foucault on power and
        surveillance 89–91
private sphere 14
Psychoanalysis and Feminism
    (Mitchell) 72
*Psychoanalysis at its Limits:
    Navigating the
    Postmodern Turn* (Elliot
    and Spezzano) 157
psychoanalytic theory
    Chodorow questions 116
    conservatism 71
    critical perspectives 166
    decentring the subject 19
    denial 25
    displacement 25
    divided self 7, 66–7
    the ego 57
    external formation of self
        10
    and feminism 26, 112–15
    feminist critique of 71–2
    Freud links unconscious with
        sexual repression 57–60
    Giddens and 49–50
    imagination and creativity
        81–2
    importance to concept of self
        162–3
    internal construction of self
        6
    Kristeva and concept of
        fantasy 120–4
    Lacan 17, 60–2, 65–6
    Lasch's narcissistic
        consumerism 78–80

psychoanalytic theory (cont.)
  little account of external,
    social conditions 70–1
  Oedipus complex 62–7, 79,
    119, 121
  and postmodernism 156–7
  repression 25
  scientific status 58–60
  social order and repression
    86
  the unconscious 10, 17, 25
  Winnicott on transitional
    relations 67–9
  Žižek's formation of identity
    82–4
  see also Freud, Sigmund
psychology
  postmodern schizophrenia
    and psychosis 147–8
psychotherapy
  conformist and oppressive
    85–6
  control of sexual behaviour
    87–8
  Foucault and social control
    110–11
  self-policing 96
  social control of sexuality
    100–3

queer theory 18, 26, 27
  formation of sexual identity
    130–3
  Foucault 98
  Fuss on identity categories
    133–4
  link to political culture 167–9
  politics and social
    transgression 132–7
  Sedgwick on language and
    social 'norms' 134–5

race and ethnicity 20
  the body 106

feminism and identity 125
identity politics 21
site of subjectivity 23
reflexivity 80, 164
  Giddens 44–50, 51–2

Regulating Bodies (Turner)
  104, 105
Reich, Wilhelm
  Character Analysis 75
  *The Mass Psychology of
    Fascism* 75
  orgone therapy 76
  psychoanalysis of politics
    75–6
repression 25
  Foucault debunks 'repressive
    hypothesis' 92–6
  Freudian concept of culture
    73–5
  Oedipus complex 62–7, 79,
    119, 121
  perceived by Reich and
    Marcuse 75–7
  and social order 86
  unconscious desires 57–60,
    165
The Reproduction of Mothering
  (Chodorow) 115–16
response cries 40
Rieff, Philip 65, 86
roles
  sex 29
  symbolically defined 33
Roman Catholicism
  confession 95–6
Rome, classical
  sexuality 96–7
Rose, Jacqueline
  critique of Chodorow
    118–19
Rose, Nikolas 107–9
  Governing the Soul 107–8
  Inventing Our Selves 107–8

Sayers, Janet 119
Schiller, Friedrich von 57
Schopenhauer, Arthur 57
The Second Sex (de Beauvoir)
    113–14
Sedgwick, Eve Kosofsky
    *The Epistemology of the
    Closet* 134–5
Segal, Lynne 119
self
    Baudrillard's concept of
        151–3
    criticism 36
    cultural assumptions 8–9
    daily routine 1–3, 5, 6
    deconstruction 17–18
    destructiveness 54
    external formation 10
    fluidity of boundaries 167
    'governmentality' 103–11
    'I' and 'me' 33–4
    identity politics 20–1, 167–9
    internal and external
        creation 10–11
    interpretation of 9–10
    love 80
    meanings 13–14
    postmodern 'death of the
        subject' 149
    psychoanalytic theory 162–3
    reflexivity 44–50, 51–2, 80
    social nature 31
    as symbolic project 9
    unity of 53–4
    various approaches to 7–12
    Žižek's concept of 82–4
Sennett, Richard 79, 144, 160
    The Corrosion of Character
        139–40
    personal effects of global
        capitalism 138–41
sexuality 13
    abuse 70–1
    bodily appearance 105–6

Butler's performative genders
    125–30
in the classical world 96–7
contemporary marriage
    46–7
contradiction 54–5
in cyberspace 141–2
Freud links unconscious and
    repression 57–60
Freudian development of
    children 59–60
medicalization of 99
Oedipus complex 62–7, 79,
    119, 121
Reich and Marcuse 75–7
'repressive hypothesis'
    debunked by Foucault
    92–6
roles 29
self-policing 95–6
site of subjectivity 23
social control 87–8, 99–103
Victorianism 93
violence 21, 102–3
Shattered Selves (Glass) 148
Situating the Self (Benhabib)
    14
Social Amnesia (Jacoby) 71
social control
    bureaucratic surveillance
        89–91
    construction of self 36–7
    Foucault on sexuality
        99–103
    order *versus* personal
        happiness 86
    by psychoanalysis 71
social theory
    concept of self 8
    double hermeneutic 11
    see also sociology
*Social Theory and
    Psychoanalysis in
    Transition* (Elliott) 162

society
  affective ways of dealing
    with others 52
  disciplines and regulates self
    8
  dislocation and
    fragmentation 79
  Goffman's performative
    behaviour 38–44
  institutions 88–9
  rapid social change 158–9
'Society as Symbolic
  Interaction' (Blumer) 34–5
sociology
  approaches 24–5
  shares symbolic meanings
    163–4
  theories of self 8
  see also social theory
Sources of the Self (Taylor) 9
Spezzano, Charles
  *Psychoanalysis at its Limits:
    Navigating the
    Postmodern Turn* (with
    Elliott) 157
'Stabat Mater' (Kristeva)
  121–2
structuralism
  language 25–6
The Subject of Modernity
  (Cascardi) 14
Subject to Ourselves (Elliott)
  158
subjectivity
  meanings 13–14
  multiple sites of 23
*The Sublime Object of
  Ideology* (Žižek) 83
surveillance
  Foucault on power and
    discipline 89–91
  Poster's communication
    technologies 106–7

symbolic interactionism 24,
  163–4
  Blumer 34–7
  Goffman and 38
  Mead 31–4, 51
  weaknesses 35–7
symbolic order
  Lacan refashions Oedipal
    complex 55–6
symbolic project 9

Taylor, Charles
  Sources of the Self 9
technology
  surveillance 106–7
  see also communications
    technology
theatre
  Goffman's metaphors of
    performance 37–44
Thinking Fragments (Flax) 72
Thomas, William I. 30
The Ticklish Subject (Žižek)
  83–4
Totem and Taboo (Freud) 73
*The Transformation of
  Intimacy* (Giddens) 44
travel
  defining self 8
Turkle, Sherry
  changeable internet identities
    141–2
  Life on the Screen 141–2
Turner, Bryan S. 106–7, 110
  The Body and Society 104
  'The Government of the
    Body' 104–5
  Regulating Bodies 104, 105
  self-regulation in postmodern
    culture 104–6
the unconscious 17, 25
  discourses and institutions
    166

divided self 7
Freud links with sexual
    repression 57–60
Lacan's splintered mirror
    145–7
lacking in symbolic
    interactionism 35–6
life and death drives 74
repressed desires 165
The Use of Pleasure (Foucault)
    96

violence
    sexual 21, 102–3

Weeks, Jeffrey 135–6
    Coming Out 131–2
Winnicott, Donald W.
    transitional relations and
        potential space 67–9

Zelig (film) 41–2
Žižek, Slavoj 25, 75,
    82–4
    on anti-Semitism 83
    identity of the self 82–4
    *The Sublime Object of
        Ideology* 83
    The Ticklish Subject 83–4